Routledge Revivals

Learning Through Interaction

Published in 1996, this book is written for teachers and other professionals who work with children with multiple disabilities. It explores and suggests ways of working with different forms of technology such as microcomputers, communications aids, multi-sensory equipment, mobility aids, and others, with children who have more than one disability. In keeping with the general aims on this book, much attention is focused on the practitioner's role in the successful use of technology.

Learning Through Interaction

Technology and Children with Multiple Disabilities

Edited by Nick Bozic and Heather Murdoch

First published in 1996
by David Fulton Publishers Ltd

This edition first published in 2018 by Routledge
2 Park Square, Milton Park, Abingdon, Oxon, OX14 4RN
and by Routledge
711 Third Avenue, New York, NY 10017

Routledge is an imprint of the Taylor & Francis Group, an informa business

© 1996 David Fulton Publishers Ltd

The right of the contributors to be identified as the authors of their work has been asserted by them in accordance with sections 77 and 78 of the Copyright, Designs and Patents Act 1988.

All rights reserved. No part of this book may be reprinted or reproduced or utilised in any form or by any electronic, mechanical, or other means, now known or hereafter invented, including photocopying and recording, or in any information storage or retrieval system, without permission in writing from the publishers.

Publisher's Note
The publisher has gone to great lengths to ensure the quality of this reprint but points out that some imperfections in the original copies may be apparent.

Disclaimer
The publisher has made every effort to trace copyright holders and welcomes correspondence from those they have been unable to contact.

A Library of Congress record exists under LCCN: 96206652

ISBN 13: 978-1-138-55138-1 (hbk)
ISBN 13: 978-1-315-14756-7 (ebk)
ISBN 13: 978-1-138-55140-4 (pbk)

David Fulton Publishers Ltd
2 Barbon Close, London WC1N 3JX

First published in Great Britain by
David Fulton Publishers 1996

Note: The right of the contributors to be identified as the authors of their work has been asserted by them in accordance with the Copyright, Designs and Patents Act 1988.

Copyright (©) David Fulton Publishers Ltd

British Library Cataloguing in Publication Data

A catalogue record for this book is available from the British Library

ISBN 1-85346-377-9

All rights reserved. No part of this publication may be reproduced, stored in a retrieval system or transmitted, in any form, or by any means, electronic, mechanical, photocopying, recording or otherwise, without the prior permission of the publishers.

Contents

Acknowledgements	iv
List of contributors	v
Foreword *Harry Daniels*	vii
1 Introduction *Nick Bozic and Heather Murdoch*	1

Part 1. Working with microcomputers

2 Joint activities and early functional communication *Nick Bozic and Chris Sherlock*	13
3 Developing information technology competencies *Tina Detheridge*	28
4 The development of early tactile reading skills *Graeme Douglas and Jean Dickens*	41
5 Optimizing the use of sensory information *Michael Tobin*	56

Part 2. Learning in technological environments

6 Social interaction in multi-sensory environments *Sheila Glenn, Cliff Cunningham and Alison Shorrock*	66
7 Developing competencies in multi-sensory rooms *Richard Hirstwood and Clive Smith*	83
8 Developing a concept of control *Leighton Reed and Christopher Addis*	92
9 Integrating the use of technology with other activities *Trevor Watts*	106

Part 3. Technology as personal tool

10 Voice Output Communication Aids *Sally Millar and Stuart Aitken*	116
11 Augmentative communication *Dithe Fisher and Clive Thursfield*	132
12 The experience of mobility *Paul Nisbet*	143
References	159
Author index	167
Subject index	169

Acknowledgements

We would like to thank Shirley Bozic and Chris Blair for their attentive proof reading; Eimei Ohshiro and Harry Daniels for helping us refine the ideas in the Introduction; and Noreen Stacey for her patient secretarial support.

Figures 12.1, 12.2, and 12.3 are reprinted from *Technology and Disability*, ISSN 1055–4181, Vol. 5 No. 1, Nisbet et al., 'Smart Wheelchairs for Mobility Training', with kind permission from Elsevier Science Ireland.

We would also like to thank Special Children for allowing us to reproduce Figure 10.5, and Macmillan Children's Books for giving us permission to quote extracts from *Peace at Last*, © 1980 Jill Murphy, in Chapter 4.

Contributors

Christopher Addis is a Teacher at the Multi-Sensory Support Unit of the Royal Schools for the Deaf, Manchester.

Dr Stuart Aitken is a Chartered Psychologist and Research Fellow at the CALL Centre, University of Edinburgh. He is also Principal Officer (Research and Practice) with Sense Scotland based in Glasgow.

Nick Bozic is a Research Fellow at the RCEVH, School of Education, University of Birmingham. He is currently funded by the RNIB.

Dr Cliff Cunningham is Visiting Professor in Applied Psychology at the School of Healthcare, Liverpool John Moores University.

Dr Harry Daniels is Professor of Special Education and Educational Psychology at the School of Education, University of Birmingham.

Tina Detheridge is a Senior Lecturer at Westminster College, Oxford. Until 1995 she was the Manager for Special Educational Needs at the National Council for Educational Technology.

Jean Dickens is a teacher of the visually impaired. Until July 1994 she worked at Rushton Hall School. She is currently doing VSO work in Indonesia.

Dr Graeme Douglas is a Research Fellow at the RCEVH, School of Education, University of Birmingham. He is currently funded by the Blatchington Court Trust.

Dithe Fisher is a Communication Therapist at the Access to Communication and Technology Department of the West Midlands Regional Rehabilitation Centre.

Dr Sheila Glenn is Head of Research and Professor of Applied Developmental Psychology at the School of Healthcare, Liverpool John Moores University.

Richard Hirstwood is a Specialist Multi Sensory Room Trainer and Advisor for Hirstwood Training.

Sally Millar is Research Fellow and Communication Therapist at the CALL Centre, University of Edinburgh.

Heather Murdoch is a lecturer in Special Education, School of Education, University of Birmingham.

Paul Nisbet is Research Fellow and Engineer with the CALL Centre, University of Edinburgh.

Leighton Reed is Teacher in Charge at the Multi Sensory Support Unit of the Royal Schools for the Deaf, Manchester.

Ms Chris Sherlock is a Specialist Speech and Language Therapist working at the Child and Family Centre, a Child Development Centre in South Birmingham which is part of the Birmingham Children's Hospital NHS Trust.

Alison Shorrock is an Occupational Therapist and Director of the SPACE Centre, Preston, Lancashire.

Clive Smith is an Advisory Teacher for children with complex learning difficulties in Lancashire.

Dr Clive Thursfield is a Consultant Clinical Scientist and Clinical Manager at the Access to Communication and Technology Department of the West Midlands Regional Rehabilitation Centre.

Dr Michael Tobin is a Reader at the School of Education, University of Birmingham. He is director of the RCEVH (Research Centre for the Education of the Visually Handicapped).

Dr Trevor Watts was the Headteacher at the Kinder Special School in Worksop, Nottinghamshire, and is now an Independent Educationalist.

Foreword

Harry Daniels

This volume is a very welcome addition to the literature on the education of children with multiple disabilities. It is distinctive by virtue of the way it seeks to discuss the mediational role of technology in functional instructional systems. In doing so it sets itself apart from some aspects of both the behavioural and developmental accounts which have had so much influence in the field. The title 'Learning through Interaction' flags this distinction. The central direction of this book is to discuss ways in which technology can help children with multiple disabilities to become active learners, rather than passive recipients of knowledge, in instructional interactions. In this way it opens possibilities for the celebration of the diversity of ways of coming to know and of new ways of engaging with the often unique educational needs of young people with very special needs.

For many years it seemed as if there were only two psychological influences in the debates about the organization of teaching and learning in the education of children with multiple disabilities. On the one hand descriptions of development were used to position learners in fairly fixed sequences of expectation and possibilities for teaching. Evidence of development was sought as a sanction for particular stages of teaching. Alternatively, instructional sequences were formulated on the basis of logical or empirical task analyses and learners were positioned in a preordained curriculum order.

Whilst these descriptions of pedagogic practice are entirely crude they serve to illustrate a fundamental concern: pupils had relatively little 'voice' in the determination of the instruction that they were to receive. By voice I am referring to the extent to which learners were seen as active constructors of their own understanding, the development of which may or may not conform to developmental or task analytic expectation. It is perhaps because of the nature of many disabilities that the combined effects of the top down and bottom up approaches have been so pervasive. An interactive pedagogy requires a subject who is willing and able to interact in a way that is understandable to the pedagogue. This book examines ways in which technology can help learners to communicate and participate in interactive learning settings with their teachers and others.

The focus on the concept of the functional system, as discussed by Bozic and Murdoch in the Introduction, positions technology in a role which is far more than that of a mere novel medium for the transmission of orthodox messages. It seeks to understand the way in which the introduction of technology into an instructional context can transform the dynamics and patterns of the communication system as well as create possibilities for participation and thus for pathways to understanding. This book may be seen as part of the movement of technology out of the pedagogic closet in which it has been in danger of languishing, either as a novel form of entertainment or as a more acceptable purveyor of dull and inert instructional systems and formats.

The editors draw on the well known concept of the Zone of Proximal Development (ZPD) which was introduced by Vygotsky (1987) in relation to both assessment and instruction. Vygotsky proposed that the distance between a child's actual developmental in a particular domain and the level reached in cooperation and with instruction from others constituted the ZPD. The general implication of the concept of this 'zone' is that at a particular stage of development, the child can tackle a certain group of tasks 'under adult guidance and in cooperation with cohorts who know more than he does', but which he cannot tackle on his own. One of Piaget's (1953a) major contributions was the emphasis he placed on individual children actively constructing their knowledge through interaction with the environment. Neo-Vygotskian writers have drawn on Piaget's concept of 'assimilation' and developed the concept of 'appropriation' (Newman et al., 1989). One of the important shifts in this conceptual move is from the model of individual to social constructivism.

Appropriation emphasizes the significance and formative influence of an individual's participation in the collective, socially significant performance of an activity. The process of internalization renders the performance of that activity individual. Interaction in the ZPD is that which enables regulation and conscious control of an activity to be transferred from teacher to learner. Hence Learning through Interaction.

It was Leont'ev (1981a) who emphasized that children have their own ways of working on learning. He suggested that they should also benefit from instruction which assists and develops this learning activity. He argued that without the influence of an appropriately structured approach to instruction, a learner will find it a struggle to learn in a way that is not hampered by the constraints of the immediate social circumstances. This is not to argue a case for instructional imposition or even to suggest the existence of an ideal instructional package or sequence. Within the Vygotskian model the appropriation process is always a two-way one. The content of instruction will be mediated and appropriated, *not* copied. Bruner used the term 'scaffolding' to describe how the more experienced tutor structures learning tasks to promote higher mental processes (Wood et al., 1976; Bruner, 1984). In Vygotsky's (1987) terms, scaffolding creates the possibilities for internalization of external knowledge as it is transformed through mediation for conscious control by the learner.

The social organization of instruction within the ZPD then becomes a central factor in the formation of individual understanding. It may be argued that the notion of 'scaffolding' tends to be associated with a one-way action supporting a preplanned scheme rather than a reciprocal interaction. My understanding of Vygotskian pedagogy is that it is dialogic in nature. Teaching involves reciprocal understanding of the intentions of instruction on the part of the pupil, and methods and outcomes of pupil learning by the teacher. If it is to be effective then these instructional dialogues must take place within the child's Zone of Proximal Development.

> The Zone of Proximal Development defines those functions that have not yet matured but are in process of maturation, functions that will mature tomorrow but are currently in an embryonic state.
>
> (Vygotsky, 1978, p.86)

The ZPD provides the setting in which the social and the individual are brought together. It is in the ZPD that the so called 'psychological tools' (particularly speech and signs) have a mediational function. A significant proportion of the literature and research associated with Vygotsky's work has concentrated on the regulative function of speech. Discussion of the means of mediation and the psychological tools which drive Vygotsky's account of the social formation of mind, has often been restricted to speech. Luria's seminal work on verbal regulation, which depicts the transfer of verbal regulation by the teacher to self-regulation, firmly directs attention onto the role of speech at the expense of other means of mediation (Luria, 1977; Luria and Yudovich, 1971). Perhaps it is for this reason that the application of Vygotsky's work to the education of pupils with multiple disabilities has been limited.

Kozulin (1990; 1986) argues that Vygotsky envisaged a theoretical programme which accounted for three types of mediator: signs and symbols (semiotic), individual activities, and interpersonal relations. The development of Vygotsky's work has revealed different degrees of emphasis on these three types or classes of mediational means. Semiotic mediation was foregrounded with reference to speech in Vygotsky's (1987) publication, *Thinking and Speech* (the retranslation of *Thought and Language*), and was discussed in relation to other systems of signs and symbols, such as sign languages, in Vygotsky (1993). He also mentioned the role of systems such as counting and algebra without engaging in a robust investigation, analysis and discussion of their operation. Vygotsky's discussion of the role of socially meaningful activity was developed at the expense of his analysis of semiotic means during the period after his death.

> The most dramatic event in the history of the concept of activity occurred in the mid 1930s when a group of Vygotsky's disciples came up with a 'revisionist' version of activity theory that put practical (material) actions at the forefront while simultaneously playing down the role of signs as mediators of human activity.
>
> (Kozulin, 1986, p. 264)

The belief developed that the structure of cognitive processes mirrored the structure of external operations. Kozulin (1986) provides an extended discussion of the tensions that arose between those who adhered to a solely activity-based semiotic account and the early Soviet psychologists who worked in the days of Stalin's influence and developed a politically correct activity-based thesis.

> Zinchenko claimed that practical activity provides a mediation between the individual and reality, whereas Vygotsky insisted that such an activity, in order to fulfil its role as a psychological tool, must necessarily be of semiotic character.
>
> (Kozulin, 1986, p.270)

The debate continues today with writers such as Engestrom (1991) doing much to re-integrate concepts of semiotic mediation within an analysis of activity.

The mediational function of interpersonal relations such as those that obtain in parenting, peer tutoring, or are characteristic of particular institutions have received relatively little attention until recently as in Tudge (1992).

Within the analysis of the semiotic mode of mediation, speech, the most powerful and pervasive of semiotic devices, functions as a psychological tool in the construction of individual consciousness. The social becomes individual not through a process of simple transmission. Individuals construct their own sense from socially-available meanings. Inner speech is the result of a constructive process whereby speech from and with others has become speech for the self. Egocentric speech, rather than being a form of thinking aloud as in the Piagetian thesis, is a transitionary phase between ordinary communicative speech and inner speech. The social voice becomes the inner voice. Changes in social circumstances (particularly patterns of communication) give rise to changes in the patterns of construction (Daniels, in press).

The very idea of mediation carries with it a number of significant implications concerning control. In that the concept denies the possibility of total control through external or internal forces it carries with it implications for instructional design and pedagogy.

> Because this auxiliary stimulus possesses the specific function of reverse action, it transfers the psychological operation to higher and qualitatively new forms and permits the humans, by the aid of extrinsic stimuli, to control their behaviour from the outside.
>
> (Vygotsky, 1978, p.40)

Vygotsky also distinguished between psychological and other tools:

> The most essential feature distinguishing the psychological tool from the technical tool, is that it directs the mind and behaviour whereas the technical tool, which is also inserted as an intermediate link between human activity and the external object, is directed toward producing one or other set of changes in the object itself.
>
> (Vygotsky, 1981, p.140)

Technology can be seen to provide technical and psychological tools. It may be used as a means of accessing modes of communication and participation or of creating new means of communication.

> As noted already, Vygotsky was stating that humans master themselves from the 'outside' through symbolic, cultural systems. What needs to be stressed here is his position that it is not the tools or signs, in and of themselves, which are important for thought development but the *meaning* encoded in them. Theoretically, then, the type of symbolic system should not matter, as long as meaning is retained. All systems (Braille for the blind and for the deaf, dactylology or finger spelling, mimicry or a natural gesticulated sign language) are tools embedded in action and give rise to meaning as such. They allow a child to internalize language and develop those higher mental functions for which language serves as the basis. In actuality, qualitatively different mediational means may result in qualitatively different forms of higher mental functioning.
>
> (Knox and Stevens, 1993, p.15, italics in original)

This book provides a number of examples of the ways in which meaning may be encoded in tools or signs provided by or made accessible by technology. The ZPD concept has been moulded and transformed to suit the purposes of a number of writers (see Lave and Wenger, 1991, chapter 2). The application of the concept to the field of multiple disability is influenced by Vygotsky's own notion of interaction and its limitations.

> We said that in collaboration the child can always do more than he can independently. We must add the stipulation that she/he cannot do infinitely more. What collaboration contributes to the child's performance is restricted to limits which are determined by the state of development and intellectual potential.
>
> (Vygotsky, 1987, p. 209)

Vygotsky was keen to remind his own audience of the need to consider and take account of the way in which biological factors come into play with cultural factors.

> the child's system of activity is determined at each specific stage both by the child's degree of organic development and by his or her degree of mastery in the use of tools.
>
> (Vygotsky cited in Tudge and Winterhoff, 1993, p.66)

> A normal child's socialization is usually fused with the process of maturation. Both series of changes converge, mutually penetrating each other to form, in essence, a single series of formative socio-biological influences on the personality.
>
> (Vygotsky cited in Tudge and Winterhoff, 1993, p.66)

The history of defectology in the former Soviet Union has been one in which children with multiple disabilities have not always been fully supported. Despite the well known centre of excellence in teaching children with multi-sensory impairment at Zagorsk, it seems as if little was done to support pupils with profound and multiple learning difficulties (Lubovsky, 1993). Whether this was for economic or other reasons is unclear.

However, in the state which witnessed at least a partial implementation of Vygotsky's ideas, much was made of his distinction between lower or natural psychological functions, such as elementary perception, memory and attention, and higher or cultural functions such as mnemonic techniques and decision making systems (Kozulin, 1986). Van der Veer and Van Ijzendoorn (1985) argue that this problem in the theoretical framework may be resolved through recent studies in Vygotskian theory which consider the possibility of demonstrating that 'natural' processes may be influenced by direction and instruction/training (see also Davydov, 1988). What is certainly required is active demonstration that what has, for very different reasons, often been thought to be impossible, is achievable. This book gives us clues as to where, with the help of technology, success might lie. Technology may help us to change attitudes. It is inescapable that Vygotsky did account for biological factors and individual differences. In his work on 'defectology' he insists that individual differences in patterns of communication give rise to differences in patterns of social mediation and hence development. Negative attitudes or lack of optimism may be more powerfully self-defeating in the education of pupils with multiple disabilities than in any other sector.

> A bodily defect is, first of all, a social and not an organic abnormality of behaviour. A bodily defect in a person causes a certain attitude towards that person among the people around him. It is this attitude, and not the defect in itself, that affects the character of psychological relations to a child with impaired sense organs.
>
> (Yaroshevsky, 1989, p.107)

However it is in the manner of social engagement that differences may arise and form their own dynamic. Vygotsky's contribution is one which should lead us to seek out and make sense of the diversity of ways of understanding and coming to understand that may exist in the population of learners with complex and multiple disabilities.

> Whatever the anticipated outcome, *always and in all circumstances*, development, complicated by a defect, represents a creative (physical and psychological) process: the creation and re-creation of a child's personality based upon the restructuring of all the adaptive functions and upon the formation of new processes – overarching, substituting, equalizing – generated by the handicap, and creating new, roundabout paths for development.
>
> (Vygotsky cited in Knox and Stevens, 1993, p.17, italics in original)

In the sense that technology can help to create a mode and means of communication it opens an important pedagogic door. This book not only discusses the ways in which pupils with multiple disabilities can be brought into better contact with their teachers; it also offers the encouragement to listen to all pupils' voices.

CHAPTER 1
Introduction

Nick Bozic and Heather Murdoch

This book is about using technology in the education of children with multiple disabilities. The term 'multiple disabilities' represents a huge range of special educational need: the children may have sensory, motor, emotional and/or intellectual impairments, in any combination. Perhaps the only common ground is the cumulative impact of multiple disabilities. A child with a visual impairment, for example, may move close to an object to examine it. A child who also has a motor impairment may not be able to use this strategy, and in this way the motor impairment effectively increases the child's visual problems. Additional learning difficulties will further impede the child's recognition of what the object is, and how it might be used. Any combination of impairments will interact in a similar way, so that the child is, in truth, multiply disabled.

Children with multiple disabilities often face enormous difficulties in understanding the world around them, controlling their environment and communicating with others. This book explores interactive approaches to helping children progress in these areas through the use of technology. *Interactive* approaches are emphasized because, too often in the past, the mystique of technology has seduced educators into believing that a technological aid or environment can benefit children solely by its presence. Leaving a child to work alone at a computer in the corner of the classroom denies the richness of the learning environment that can be created by educator, child and technology together.

The book is divided into three sections, each considering a different type or usage of technology, and each presenting a series of ideas and accounts of practice. The chapters in the first section deal with the use of microcomputers. The second section considers the way in which technology can be used to create learning environments. Finally, the third section looks at the use of technology as a tool, which children can take with them between environments. This introduction examines the concepts underlying the approaches described in the rest of the book, and uses examples from later chapters to illustrate a model of the processes involved in using technology with children with multiple disabilities.

Functional systems

A fundamental theme of the book is that children's learning activities are *mediated* through their interactions with:

- Technology
- Educators.

(This interaction is shown in Figure 1.1.) Typically, the activities of the child, technology and educator form what has been called a *functional system* (Anokhin, 1969; Luria, 1979; Newman et al., 1989; Crook, 1994). That is, their activity in combination realizes a goal.

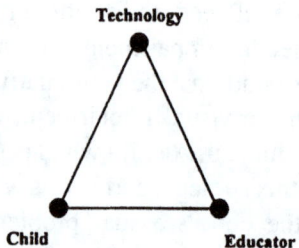

Figure 1.1: The functional system of child, technology, and educator

Examples of this structure can be found throughout the book. Douglas and Dickens (Chapter 4), for example, describe a functional system in which child, technology and teacher interact to achieve the shared goal of reading words in the tactile Moon script.

The switching system designed by Reed and Addis (Chapter 8), to give children the experience of control, can also be viewed as a functional system. Here the goal of the system is simpler: to give the child opportunities to trigger events. In this example, the interlocking activities of child, technology and teacher are seen to spread over a longer time span. By collecting information about the child, and selecting appropriate apparatus, the teacher makes a vital contribution to the functional system, perhaps days before the technology is actually used.

Each chapter of the book describes educators creating a functional system that is tailored to the needs of an individual child. Vygotsky's (1978) concept of the Zone of Proximal Development (ZPD) helps to explain the potential benefits achieved by this process.

The Zone of Proximal Development

The Zone of Proximal Development represents the range of activities which a child can accomplish with support from an adult or more competent child. Vygotsky claims that it provides an optimal way of thinking about a child's abilities, in that it addresses not only what the child can currently do independently, but also the range of skills which s/he is on the verge of mastering. He writes:

> In collaboration, the child solves problems that are proximal to his level of development with relative ease. Further on, however, the difficulty grows. Ultimately, problems become too difficult to resolve even in collaboration. The child's potential for moving from what he can do to what he can do only in collaboration is the most sensitive index of the dynamics of development and the degree of success that will come to characterize the child's mental activity.
>
> (Vygotsky, 1987, p.210)

The ZPD is an important concept in teaching and learning, not least because of the idea of *internalization* (Vygotsky, 1981; Wertsch, 1985). Vygotsky's use of this term differs from Piaget's: Vygotsky believes that performing an activity in a social context is a necessary precursor to performing it independently. He sees collaboration with a more competent other in a joint activity as leading the child towards internalization of the methods used to achieve the goal. Over time, and with repeated performance, the child is able to achieve these ends independently. In Vygotsky's words:

> What a child can do with assistance today she will be able to do by herself tomorrow.
>
> (Vygotsky, 1978, p.87)

The teaching/learning process is therefore viewed as one of apprenticeship. Through successive cycles of an activity, the more competent adult gradually hands over responsibility for the achievement of the goal to the child.

The notion of a *functional system*, discussed above, is related to the concept of the Zone of Proximal Development because functional systems provide children with supportive contexts that enable them to operate within their ZPDs. This book contains many examples of the use of technology to provide this kind of supportive context for children with multiple disabilities. Common to all of these is the assumption that the total learning experience cannot be reduced to either the role of the educator, or child, or technology, in isolation. It is their interaction which forms the basis for learning.

A cyclical model for using technology

The educator plays a crucial role in mediating the child's use of technology, by creating and developing the functional system that will allow the child to work within his or her ZPD. The educator's mediating influence can be represented by a cyclical model showing the typical sequence of tasks: deciding valid aims for the functional system; planning its operation; managing the intervention of the functional system; and finally reviewing its success.

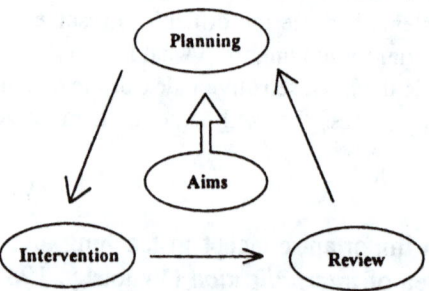

Figure 1.2: A cyclical approach to the use of educational technology

The model shown in Figure 1.2 is designed to allow practitioners to evaluate how best to use technology in their own educational setting, and the chapters of this book illustrate its use. As the model can be applied to any form of technology, it will not date as existing technologies become obsolete. The four stages of the model are considered below in greater detail, and illustrated by examples from chapters within this book.

Aims of a functional system

The aims of using technology should be educationally led, rather than led by the technology itself. Within this book there are examples of technology being used for a variety of educational aims (for example, to improve communicative abilities; as an aid to developing functional vision; working towards literacy).

A number of points are relevant. Firstly, it is important that the aims of a functional system are sufficiently ambitious to fall within the child's ZPD. The co-ordinated activity of educator, technology and child should focus on tasks which the child currently cannot perform unaided. So Detheridge (Chapter 3) describes how, with adult support and suitable microcomputer software, a child can be encouraged to make choices where before they did not.

On the other hand, the aims of the functional system must not be in advance of what the child can reasonably perform with the assistance of others. Some problems will be too difficult for the child, however great the degree of collaboration. The aims need to be chosen to stretch a child to the right level, but not beyond.

This leads to the idea that the aims may be divided into a series of objectives, some of which are attained before others. Nisbet (Chapter 12) demonstrates how the global aim of using 'intelligent' wheelchairs in order to give children the experience of mobility can be divided into a series of individualized objectives. A child first learns how to control simple movement (forwards using a finger switch), and later learns how to control the motion of the wheelchair in more complex ways, such as stopping and turning.

This example highlights one of the most exciting aspects of using technology with children with multiple disabilities: aims that would not otherwise be possible can be made so, with the careful introduction of technological support. The child's Zone of Proximal Development can in effect be *extended* by the introduction of appropriate technology to the functional systems that constitute the child's experience of the world.

Planning a functional system

Once the aims have been selected, the educator needs to set up a functional system which works towards their attainment. The first step in this process is to consider the two other components of the functional system: the child and the technology.

The child

Even where the aims of an activity are similar for two or more children, different individuals will bring their own combinations of abilities and preferences, and may benefit from functional systems with differentially organized components. An initial assessment of the child is, therefore, essential.

Vygotsky's concept of the ZPD suggests that there are two relevant indicators of development. These are:

> the actual developmental level as determined by [the child's] independent problem solving, and the level of potential development as determined through problem solving under adult guidance or in collaboration with more capable peers.
>
> (Vygotsky, 1978, p.86)

From this viewpoint, assessment of children's abilities requires more than the measurement of their actual (or current) developmental level, although this is valuable. There is also a need to identify what children are able to achieve with support (Brown and Ferrara, 1985; Lunt, 1993).

The authors of this book approach the problem in different ways. Some restrict their assessment of children to their actual developmental levels. Others try to get an idea of a child's potential. Detheridge (Chapter 3), for instance, argues that the support of information technology is particularly effective in allowing children to demonstrate otherwise 'hidden competencies', although its deployment for this purpose needs careful management.

Fisher and Thursfield (Chapter 11) discuss the assessment of a child's communicative abilities prior to the provision of a communication aid. They describe how detailed discussion between parents and professionals can help to generate a realistic picture of a child's potential abilities. Different people in the child's life may have expectations of a child's ability which are either too low or too high. This may be because the child operates differently in different contexts, perhaps only extending him- or herself in particular social settings.

Fisher and Thursfield emphasize that all those involved with the child should have a similar level of expectation regarding the child's potential ability in future functional systems:

> Within the group, there may be significant differences in expectations, reflecting discrepancies in perceptions of the child's ability and potential. If these are not addressed, the group will not be able to work as a team.

The issue of motivation is worth considering. The functional system which is developed needs to motivate and interest the child for whom it is designed. Reed and Addis (Chapter 8) describe how they assess a child to establish the kinds of things s/he enjoys. Again the importance of individualized programmes comes across strongly:

> We have to know what the child likes, and all children are different. It goes without saying that some children love a footspa whilst others do not.

A similar concern with motivation assessment is articulated in other chapters. For example, Fisher and Thursfield (Chapter 11) discuss the way that descriptions of children's daily routines can often shed light on their likes and dislikes. Such information has real practical relevance for setting up appropriate functional systems to support the introduction of communication aids.

The technology

In planning a functional system, teachers need to consider how the child's learning is to be mediated by technology. What are the potential advantages of using technology, rather than other educational media, in the pursuit of particular aims? Answering this question will involve assessing the potential benefits that various technologies afford (Wertsch, 1995; Crook, 1994).

In Chapter 5, Tobin describes how children with multiple disabilities and visual impairment were able to read a much smaller print size when text was presented on a computer screen, rather than the printed page. The computer seemed to extend these children's abilities. However, there has been debate about whether the notion of 'amplification' (Bruner, 1966) is sufficient to characterize the benefits of using technology to mediate learning. Technology can allow children to achieve more, but in reorganizing the way that activities are carried out (Cole and Griffin, 1980; Crook, 1994) it can create the possibility for qualitatively new experiences. For example, both Millar and Aitken (Chapter 10) and Fisher and Thursfield (Chapter 11), illustrate the way in which communication aids can provide children with the means to develop communication skills (the ability to request, refuse, command etc.) which they would otherwise not acquire.

Elsewhere within this book a similar structural impact on activities is evident. Tobin (Chapter 5) describes how the introduction of microcomputer technology transformed Nicholl into an active learner who could control screen-based events and signal choices.

Similarly, Watts (Chapter 9) outlines the process by which the introduction of switch-controlled technology can add a new dimension to children's leisure activities. In the case study he describes, a previously passive child was provided with reasons to initiate communication with other children and staff.

Teachers need to consider carefully the way in which technological mediation is likely to influence the structure of educational activities. Bozic and Sherlock (Chapter 2), for example, discuss the use of a microcomputer in communication development. Their chosen software offers a repeatable sequence of discrete events, allowing the child to build up anticipation, and giving the adult control of the timing of the sequence. Software designed to drill specific responses, with the computer controlling the shift from one step to the next, would create a quite different functional system.

This point is especially important given Vygotsky's concept of internalization. This suggests that the nature of the functional system (the way in which technology is used by the educator and child together) has a shaping effect on the child's conceptual development.

However, although every piece of technology affords a range of more or less likely uses, it never determines the exact nature of that use (Wertsch, 1995). For example, Millar and Aitken (Chapter 10) describe how Taction Pads – small pads which talk when they are pressed – can be programmed with a variety of different messages depending on the needs of individual learners. Bozic and Sherlock (Chapter 2) use software to develop communication skills, but the same programs might well be used in a visual stimulation session (see Tobin, Chapter 5). Acting creatively, educators can generate new ways of using technology – new functional systems involving the technology, educator and child – to support appropriate educational aims.

Sometimes the available technology needs to be moulded to support specific activities. In their chapter on multi-sensory rooms, Hirstwood and Smith (Chapter 7) describe the rearrangement of one room in order to provide a child with an environment in which he could relax. The soft play flooring that normally provides children with a safe, cushioned surface disadvantaged this child, by accentuating his mobility problems, and the room was adapted for his needs by moving and reversing the floor covering.

The concept keyboard overlays described by Douglas and Dickens (Chapter 4) were designed to support a joint reading activity. A tactile path on each overlay provides a sustained focus for joint attention, and sound-buttons along the path give teacher and child the opportunity to attend to specific reading-related tasks (for example, deriving phonemes from letters and understanding the meaning of sentences).

Intervention: the functional system in action

This section considers the functional system in action, and again highlights the importance of the educator's role – this time in supporting the child to ensure that tasks are completed successfully. The child's role, however, is by no means a passive one, and includes initiating events and acting creatively within the format of the functional system.

Scaffolding action

Wood et al. (1976) introduce the notion of 'scaffolding' to explain how a more competent adult can support a child's achievement of a task. Essentially, the adult acts to provide assistance when it is most needed (when the child is struggling). As the child's competence grows, the adult gradually provides less support.

Scaffolding, then, is a method of encouraging a child to work within his or her Zone of Proximal Development. There are many examples of the process within this book. Douglas and Dickens (Chapter 4), for example, analyze in detail the scaffolding provided by a teacher to support a child's accomplishment of a concept keyboard reading task. Detheridge (Chapter 3) explains how the child's use of a computer to make choices can be facilitated by:

> the teacher ... moving the indicating pointer in response to the attention and understanding of the pupil, but leaving time for the pupil to make a selection when s/he wishes. The important purpose, of the pupil making and indicating a choice, can in this way be achieved through co-operation.

This example illustrates the sharing of responsibility for the achievement of goals. This sharing is facilitated by the idea that any activity is made up of a series of *actions* (Leont'ev, 1981b). While the child operates at a relatively low level of competence, the teacher takes responsibility for most of the necessary actions. Later, as the child becomes more capable, the balance of responsibility shifts in his or her direction.

Interestingly, within a functional system of child, educator and technology, the responsibility for scaffolding the child's progress is not restricted to the educator. The technology can also be seen to perform a scaffolding function, *albeit through the careful management of the teacher*. For example, Nisbet (Chapter 12) discusses the way in which Smart Wheelchairs are systematically configured to offer particular forms of mobility activity. Initially a chair is configured so that a child can only perform basic activities, such as moving forwards. At this stage, the chair itself is programmed to take responsibility for more complex manoeuvres. Later, the chair is successively reconfigured to provide the more competent child with increasing control over his or her movement.

Similarly, the technology of Reed and Addis's (Chapter 8) switching systems is used to scaffold the child's mastery of cause-effect. Initially the technology is arranged so that it is triggered by the child's slightest movement. The responsibility for performing a triggering action, in other words, is minimized by the arrangement of the equipment. Reed and Addis describe a number of methods for reducing the level of scaffolding, to encourage children to extend their repertoire of triggering actions.

Child-led activities

Cole and Griffin (1984) warn that the notion of scaffolding risks leaving little room for children's creativity. Goals, and actions to achieve them, may potentially be pre-specified by the teacher to the extent that the child's role is solely one of compliance. In this book, Glenn, Cunningham and Shorrock (Chapter 6) echo the concern with regard to children with multiple disabilities:

> The emphasis is frequently on teacher-selected, goal-oriented activities which are often then teacher-led, and this in turn is likely to reduce child control and spontaneity.

Glenn et al. discuss ways of using multi-sensory rooms as vehicles for encouraging child-led activities. Even in the situations they describe, however, adult scaffolding is required to create the conditions in which children can exercise choice and initiative. The adult's contribution should not be seen as devaluing the child's input. Children with multiple disabilities, like other children, need opportunities actively to shape the way events unfold. They must have a means of influencing the workings of the functional system of which they are a part.

Children are more likely to be motivated when they have a stake in the activity. For example, Millar and Aitken (Chapter 10), in their discussion of message design for communication aids, stress that children's use of technology must deliver 'real' choices:

> [I]t is important not to display choices which cannot realistically be 'delivered' immediately. If children do attempt to choose but are fobbed off with 'oh yes, we'll be going swimming next Wednesday'; or 'you'll get a drink after dinner', even the most severely disabled children quickly learn that this was not a true choice but an empty exercise with no apparent pay-off for them, and they will stop cooperating with the activity.

In this example, children's ability to control their social environment is scaffolded by the creation of appropriate message structures and adult responses. The example illustrates the concept of scaffolding as a tool to empower children, rather than restrict their agency.

Reviewing the functional system

As the child's competence grows, the educator transfers more and more responsibility for the running of the functional system to the child. Ultimately, however, this is not enough. Through learning, the child's Zone of Proximal Development has changed, and hence an activity that previously stretched the child no longer does so, because the child is now more able. The fourth stage of the cyclical model is that of *review*. The educator needs to review the success (or otherwise) of the functional system, and modify its arrangement, so that the child once again works within his or her current ZPD.

The cyclical review-oriented approach to the use of technology with children with multiple disabilities is emphasized in many of the chapters in this book. Watts (Chapter 9), for instance, describes a cyclical model involving decisions and goal setting, preparation, intervention and recording, and evaluation. The next cycle of the functional system may involve the creation of new aims, fresh assessments and a new organization for the functional system. Evans (1993) argues that this kind of approach captures the dynamic way in which educators ensure children continue to work within their ZPDs.

Fisher and Thursfield (Chapter 11) outline the process that they go through when they review the success of an intervention. They highlight the range of factors that must be considered if the planned objectives have not been attained:

> Was the plan carried out as agreed? Did all the equipment work as it should? Were there unexpected disruptions; illness, staff absence, family troubles? If there is no obvious external problem, perhaps the step was too ambitious; could it be broken down further? This cycle of goal setting, intervention and review continues until a satisfactory end is reached.

If the objectives have been attained, the next cycle of activity may aim to develop the child's abilities in new environments – to move towards a more generalized level of attainment. Watts (Chapter 9) discusses the initial siting of a functional system within a highly controllable environment, where distractions can be kept to a minimum. The artificial environment acts as a scaffolding influence, making it easier for the child to attend to salient events. In this context, the move to a new environment 'will often be a measure of progress in itself.'

Reed and Addis (Chapter 8) discuss the ways in which their work with switching systems may be generalized into the home or care environment. Appropriate goals with similarities to those achieved through the child's switching system are identified, and new functional systems are devised in which parents or carers work with children towards these goals.

Conclusion

The aim of this introduction has been to provide a model for practitioners working with children with multiple disabilities, and implementing new technologies within their own settings. The model takes the form of a cyclical framework based on the concept of functional systems. It describes a commonality of approach – learning as the outcome of a series of different forms of interaction – but does not imply uniformity in the way the ideas are applied. The framework can be used to support a diverse range of applications meeting different special needs.

The chapters which follow illustrate both the commonality and the diversity described above. They present and evaluate a wide range of practical applications of direct relevance to those working with children with multiple disabilities.

Part I
Working with microcomputers

CHAPTER 2
Joint activities and early functional communication

Nick Bozic and Chris Sherlock

Introduction

Functional communication skills help children achieve particular goals within their social environment. For example, developmental psychologists claim that one of the earliest communicative functions that a (sighted) child learns is how to signal to an adult that they want an object, by reaching for it despite the fact that it is actually out of reach (Bruner, 1975).

This chapter describes how microcomputers can be used as the basis for joint activities in order to develop the early functional communication skills of children with multiple disabilities. Readers are introduced to an approach and provided with guidance on its implementation.

The chapter is divided into four sections. In the first section there is a brief discussion of the educational and psychological research from which the approach stems.

The second section deals with choosing an appropriate joint activity. It describes how a child might be assessed in order to gauge the range of functional communication skills s/he possesses, and how this process may relate to the choice of a joint activity.

In the third section, four joint activities are introduced as vehicles for the expression of particular sets of communicative functions. The type of software used is described, and case studies are presented to give concrete examples of each activity in practice.

Finally, the fourth section discusses some of the issues that arise in the practice of joint activity based work. Attention is drawn to the ways in which both adult and child can act to change the course of an activity. Particular importance is attributed to the role of interpretation in the development of shared meaning.

Theoretical and educational context

Psychological research (e.g. Bruner, 1978, 1983; Snow, 1989) has highlighted the way that joint activities between adult and child can provide a flexible and motivating context for the child's acquisition of communication and language skills. Joint activities are, often, very simple, game-like routines – for example, an adult might blow bubbles and a child burst them with her finger; or an adult and child might roll a ball to one another.

Several features of joint activities make them well suited for children who are operating at a prelinguistic or minimally linguistic level of communication, and these are outlined below. These features have also meant that joint activities are often exploited in language and communication intervention work with children who have learning and other disabilities (e.g. Bozic, 1995; Coupe et al., 1988; Kim and Lombardino, 1991).

Halle (1984) points out that joint activities can provide a child with genuine reasons to communicate with the other person involved. This contrasts with less naturalistic approaches that do not site communication interventions within meaningful activity (Goldbart, 1988a).

In addition, Snyder-McLean et al. (1984) point to the following four advantages of joint activities (or joint action routines as they call them). Joint activities provide:

- A limited range of possible meanings, making low demands on a child's comprehension and expression.
- A repetitive and therefore predictable sequence of events, giving the child time to anticipate what will happen next and formulate an intention to communicate.
- Scope for novelty and new communicative aims.
- A restricted 'world' which makes the child's responses more easily interpretable by the adult.

These are factors which may easily be absent from a child's social world unless they are specifically built into it.

Computer-based joint activities

In this chapter we demonstrate how microcomputers can form the focus for joint activities with young children who have multiple disabilities. This approach has developed out of earlier work with children with visual impairments and/or learning difficulties (see Bozic, 1993; Bozic, 1995; Bozic et al., 1995). It requires only the simplest of switch-operated software, and can be used to promote the communication skills of children at very early stages of language/communication development.

Microcomputers offer three distinct advantages in relation to joint activities and children with multiple disabilities. With the right software they:

- Provide the base structure for a joint activity – appropriate software can offer a repeatable sequence of events which can be woven into (and help give substance to) a joint activity between an adult and a child.
- Can be used to optimize the sensory environment – they provide the adult partner with the ability to choose a visual and/or auditory context that will suit the child's perceptual abilities.
- Can give children with limited motor skills the opportunity to control events – switches, touchscreens and other input devices can make things easier to control.

Despite these advantages, the use of microcomputers should form only one aspect of a complete intervention programme. Overall, the child's communicative abilities should be fostered across a range of different settings, and with different participants, throughout the day (Harris, 1990), to support the generalization of skills.

Aims

Our work uses microcomputer-based intervention to help young children with multiple disabilities develop early *functional* communication skills.

In our work we aimed to nurture some of the functions of communication that in normal development begin to be present at 9 to 12 months of age (Halliday, 1975). We used the categories of early functional communication provided by a well known British checklist, the *Pre-Verbal Communication Schedule (PVCS)* (Kiernan and Reid, 1987a, 1987b) to specify the kinds of abilities we wanted to promote. Microcomputer-based joint activities were then designed in order to provide 'naturally occurring' reasons for the expression of these functions.

In practice we used only four of the six categories that the PVCS provides:

- **Simple Negation**: The child acts to refuse or reject something.
- **Need Satisfaction**: The child communicates in order to satisfy a need.
- **Positive Interaction**: The child interacts in a positive manner with others (e.g. greeting, expressions of emotion)
- **Shared Attention**: The child communicates in order to draw another

person's attention to something, but without intending to satisfy a need.

The two functions we omitted were Attention Seeking and Negative Interaction: Attention Seeking because it only relates to the self rather than other objects (such as computers); and Negative Interaction because it represents a set of 'problem behaviours' rather than a desirable function of communication (Kiernan, 1988).

The PVCS categories emerged from work with children with severe learning difficulties. It would, of course, have been entirely feasible to base our work around a different model of early functional communication, for example Halliday's (1975) scheme or the one provided by the Pragmatics Profile (Dewart and Summers, 1988). However, the PVCS categories share many similarities with other categorizations of early functional communication (for a fuller discussion of this issue see Goldbart, 1988a). They seem to offer a model appropriate for children with a range of needs, and as such to form a suitable basis for our work.

Choosing an appropriate joint activity

We begin by describing some of the prerequisites for this type of intervention. We then outline our approach to assessing a child's functional communication skills, and introduce the four different microcomputer-based joint activities developed to promote these skills.

Prerequisites

We would expect normally developing children to respond to microcomputer-based joint activities from the final quarter of their first year, as at this time they begin to co-ordinate their actions towards objects and people (Astington, 1994). Some children with multiple disabilities will demonstrate readiness by similar behaviours to nondisabled children, albeit at a later age. For example, the child may follow an adult's line of regard to see what s/he is looking at, or may reach for an object out of reach, to indicate that s/he would like to play with it.

If the child has a visual impairment severely affecting the ability to see distant objects, however, the 'milestone' behaviours mentioned above may not be relevant (Urwin, 1983). In this case we need to look for 'parallel developments' (Urwin, ibid., p.149), in which children demonstrate their ability to interact with others' actions in relation to objects in near space. We may also look for gestures that serve as signals, but are based on actions performed with objects, rather than reaching behaviour (Rogow, 1980).

Assessment of the child

If a child displays signs of being able to co-ordinate his or her attention between objects and people, the next step is to assess the extent to which s/he uses communication for any of the functions previously described. Alternatively, if the child has not reached this stage it may still be worth doing some basic work around the computer to encourage the development of joint attention (see the Attending Together Activity).

An assessment of a child's functional communication skills may be carried out by interviewing parents and other carers, and by observing the child in a variety of situations – for example, during unstructured play activities or at mealtimes. On these occasions, other people should be nearby, and the child should have some reason to communicate. The child's communication (using spoken words, gestures, vocalizations or other behaviours) should be recorded and analyzed: How often does s/he communicate? By what means? How consistently? What categories of communication (simple negation, need satisfaction etc.) are used?

For some children it may be best to use a published assessment schedule – for example, the Pre-Verbal Communication Schedule (Kiernan and Reid, 1987a,b), or the Pragmatics Profile (Dewart and Summers, 1988) – to assess their functional communication skills.

Selecting a joint activity

When a child's current range of communicative functions is known, it is possible to select an appropriate joint activity. Adult partners may wish to select an activity intended to consolidate a child's use of a particular communicative function, and/or to develop one that is not currently in the child's repertoire.

The joint activities

Table 2.1 presents four microcomputer-based joint activities and the range of communicative functions which they give a child the opportunity to express.

Joint Activities	Communicative Functions			
	Need Satisfaction	Simple Negation	Positive Interaction	Shared Attention
Attending Together		X		
Make it Change!	X	X		
Look at This!		X		X
Pretend Friend	X	X	X	X

Table 2.1: Four joint activities

The four microcomputer-based joint activities (which we describe in more detail below), were designed according to a set of criteria culled from relevant research in the area (see Table 2.2).

Below, for each activity, we outline:
- The communicative functions which it promotes.
- The type of software and computer hardware required to put it into practice.
- The basic structure of the activity.
- A case study giving a concrete example of the activity in practice.

- An activity should present opportunities and motivation for the child to communicate the target function.

- An activity should have a clear structure: a beginning and an end, etc. (Kiernan et al., 1987).

- Ideally the roles of the adult and child should be reciprocal (i.e. complementary) (Newson, 1993) and possibly reversible.

- The child's focus of attention should be controlled by the natural flow of the activity rather than extrinsically imposed rules (Bozic, 1995).

- While expecting that developmentally young children may be able to appreciate another person's wants/needs and some basic emotions, we sought to avoid putting them in positions where they would have to understand more sophisticated notions about a person's intentions (Astington, 1994).

Table 2.2: Criteria for the design of joint activities

Attending Together

This fundamental activity provides a structure within which the basic joint attention skills (prerequisites for a child's participation in later joint activity work) can be improved and developed. In common with the other activities, it offers a context within which the child can make the functional act of Simple Negation.

This joint activity seems suited to what may be called single-event software. With this type of program a switch press triggers a single 'happening'. For example, the image of a firework might burst across the screen while an exploding sound is played through the computer's loudspeakers.

At the beginning of a typical Attending Together activity the child and adult sit facing the computer monitor. The screen is blank. The adult waits for the child's attention to focus on the screen, if necessary tapping the screen gently to guide the child's gaze towards the monitor. Then s/he presses a switch (or hits a key on the keyboard) to trigger the event.

This is the moment when the child may become aware that both s/he and the adult partner are jointly attending to what has appeared on the screen. It is vital that the adult imbues the event with suitable emotional meaning – perhaps by vocalizing 'aah!' or 'ooh!'. Ideally the image/sound should continue changing until it finally disappears, thus extending the time available for shared attention.

As in all computer-based joint activities the child should be given opportunities to indicate that they would like to stop and do something else (Simple Negation). This can be achieved by asking simple questions (e.g. 'Shall we do it again?'), and richly interpreting any response the child makes. For instance, in this context turning in the chair to look elsewhere might be interpreted as a sign that the child has had enough.

Case study

Tom was aged one year and six months. He had Down's Syndrome and a mild to moderate hearing impairment. His communication skills were delayed and he was only just beginning to co-ordinate his attention between objects and people. Although he had two or three vocalizations he did not use them meaningfully.

We began the **Attending Together** activity by using a piece of software which produced the image and sound of a helicopter when the adult pressed a switch. The helicopter would appear and then 'fly up' and disappear off the top of the screen.

Although the program allowed other images to be displayed in a similar way (cars, trains, etc.), the helicopter seemed to be the best at holding Tom's attention. We attributed this to the low frequency sound it made as it flew away – Tom found it easier to hear low-pitched noise.

Each session with Tom lasted about seven or eight minutes. His mother and the speech and language therapist cued Tom to expect the helicopter with appropriate comments. When it arrived they said 'ahh!' in a tone of wonderment. However during the first session Tom found it more interesting to look at the adults at this point, rather than to share the focus of their attention.

In subsequent sessions there was more vocalization from Tom, especially more shared vocalization on the appearance of an image: 'aahh!' Tom also showed an ability to alternate his attention between adult and computer.

Throughout these sessions the therapist used gesture and language to enquire whether Tom had had enough. Any wriggling or turning in his seat was taken as an indication that Tom wished to finish the activity (Simple Negation), and acted on accordingly.

Make it Change!

The aim of this activity is to develop the child's ability to express needs or wants (i.e. the Need Satisfaction function of communication). It works well with single-event software.

Initially this activity is the same as the Attending Together activity. The adult partner repeatedly works through the activity, so that the child gets used to what happens. S/he builds up the suspense and anticipation of the event, and excitement at its fulfilment, through suitable accompanying gestures and 'motherese' commentary ('What's going to happen now?'; 'Ooh look at that!', etc.).

When the child has become accustomed to what happens during each cycle of the activity, the adult partner delays triggering the event by slightly pausing before s/he presses the switch. This pause provides the opportunity for the child to request the event (Need Satisfaction).

Here the adult looks to shape any signal that the child produces towards a more clearly communicative form. Ideally the child actively communicates with the adult in order to get something to happen, rather than mechanically behaving in a way which s/he has learnt will bring about a desired outcome.

Case study

Charlotte was aged one year and eight months. She had a visual impairment causing nystagmus, hypotonia and moderate learning difficulties. Her functional communication was limited in that she responded indiscriminately to other people's utterances – she knew a handful of first words, but used them without any sense of purpose. Charlotte was poor at anticipating people's simple communicative actions, and did little to initiate interaction. She did, however, have the ability to attend jointly to events with another person and we aimed to build on this, to move her towards more purposeful communication.

With Charlotte we used a single-event program that produced interesting patterns on the touch of a switch. The speech and language therapist adapted the **Make it Change!** activity using the phrase 'Ready, Steady, Go'. She cued Charlotte with 'Ready, Steady' and then paused before saying 'Go', hoping that Charlotte would say it herself, or make an equivalent gesture or vocalization.

When the activity was first tried, Charlotte said 'Oh' when the therapist said 'Go', and reached out with her hand to touch the therapist's head. On later occasions, when the therapist paused after saying 'Ready, Steady', Charlotte patted the screen with both hands, while looking at the therapist from time to time, and this was interpreted as a signal to trigger the pattern.

There was an interval when Charlotte did not make signals that could be interpreted as demands to press the switch. Instead she made a blowing sound and the therapist responded by copying her, and saying 'Yes, it's boring, isn't it!' (By recognizing a communicative behaviour, the therapist generated a slice of positive interaction.)

The Ready, Steady, Go variant of **Make it Change!** has its own distinctive feel. It seems to be particularly good for developing the child's receptive communication skills, and ability to time contributions in a simple dialogue. At the time of writing, if Charlotte says 'Go' she tends to say it whenever she hears the therapist say 'Ready', rather than waiting for the right moment.

Look at This!

This activity attempts to create a situation where the child is encouraged to redirect the adult's attention to an interesting event, and so communicate the Shared Attention function.

We based this activity around what we called sequence software – programs that produced repetitive sequences of two or more events, each event triggered by the press of a switch. So, for example, a typical sequence program might build a picture in blocks – each press of the switch adding a block until the picture is complete.

For a period of time adult and child repeat the sequence with the adult elaborating the significance of events with various comments. It is important that the child becomes used to the repetitive nature of the experience, so that later they will be surprised by a change.

When the child is anticipating what will happen next – both in terms of the computer-generated events and the adult's reaction to them, the adult manipulates the situation to provide some kind of 'unexpected event' (McClenny et al, 1992). For example, the adult might turn away while an interesting part of the sequence is presented; or they might manipulate the software so that it produces an unexpected sequence (for example, a new image).

The idea is that the unexpected event will provoke the child to a communicative act aimed at (re)directing the adult's attention. At the point when the unexpected event occurs, it is important that the adult allows the child enough time to formulate a communicative action.

Case study

Bradley was aged two years and seven months. He had cerebral atrophy and moderate learning difficulties. At the start of the study Bradley had about 50 words. His functional use of these was mainly limited to naming, and he was generally very passive. For this reason we decided to try and develop his ability to demand Shared Attention and used the **Look at This!** activity with him.

With Bradley the speech and language therapist used a sequence program, in which one press of a switch made a cartoon character rise up from behind a wall, and a second press made him drop down again. The therapist spent some time getting Bradley used to this sequence of events, accompanying each with suitable verbal/gestural commentary ('Up he comes!', 'Let's make him go down again.').

Then, on one occasion, as the cartoon rose up and Bradley expected the therapist to maintain joint attention with him, she remained silent and looked away to give him the impression that she wasn't attending.

The disadvantage of this strategy was that, having looked away, the therapist was unable to see whether Bradley was making any efforts to communicate with her (a mirror would have been useful). The presence of Bradley's mother helped at this point, as she drew the therapist's attention to any movement or vocalization that could be interpreted as a request from Bradley.

In fact Bradley vocalized to indicate that he wanted the therapist to look round again. He made a 'Ssshh' sound which the therapist interpreted as approximating to the final syllable of her name. However, it would appear that at this stage Bradley is only imitating his mother's modelling of the therapist's name. Over time the therapist aims to use this joint activity to develop Bradley's ability to direct her attention, perhaps through touching, looking round at her face or vocalizing.

Pretend Friend

In the Pretend Friend activity we were intent on providing the child with opportunities to engage in Positive Interaction, defined as communication about feelings, the expression of greetings and leave-takings etc.

We based our approach on alternating-sequence software: programs that alternated between producing one of two sequences of events. Each event in a sequence was triggered by the press of a switch. So, for example, the first sequence of switch presses might play the tune 'Baa baa black sheep', and after this pressing the switch would play the next sequence, perhaps 'Here we go round the mulberry bush'.

The activity itself is a form of pretend play and utilizes emotional states which developmentally young children can often understand. With appropriate facial expressions, gestures and commentary, the adult pretends that s/he doesn't like the content of one of the sequences, but is overjoyed to hear and/or see the content of the other. S/he leaves plenty of time between switch presses to allow the child to respond to his or her positive/negative emotional state.

To add a greetings/leave-takings dimension the sequences can represent the coming and going of characters. For example, the sound of somebody opening a door and saying 'Hello', or the sound of footsteps walking away and someone saying 'Goodbye'. Again, utterances can be imbued with appropriate emotional content: happiness on arrival, sorrow on departure.

Case study

Daniel was aged one year and seven months. He had a neuronal migrational disorder which had led to a series of learning difficulties, including some visual problems – typically he seemed 'slow to see'. The speech and language therapist estimated that Daniel's communication skills were delayed by around six months. He knew a few words but used these in a rather passive stimulus-response type manner. The therapist was interested in getting Daniel to become more active and take more initiative in interactions.

We tried the **Pretend Friend** activity using an extended version of the software described in the **Look at This** case study. This time, in the first sequence a Blob-type character rose up from behind a wall, and then in a second sequence a teddy bear rose up from behind the wall.

The therapist pretended she didn't like the Blob-type character, screwing up her face and saying things like 'Urgh! I don't like Blob, take him away'. When Teddy appeared, however, she smiled and said 'I like Teddy, isn't he nice?' During each sequence she made sure that between switch presses there was time for Daniel to respond to her reactions.

When the therapist said that she didn't like Blob, and made appropriate facial expressions of dislike, Daniel smiled and pointed at the screen. He also smiled when Teddy appeared. The therapist felt that he understood and enjoyed the pretend nature of the activity, and that in later sessions they would be able to build on this foundation – for example, that if she turned away, Daniel might (gleefully) redirect her attention back to the disliked character.

Interestingly, later on in this session, instead of Blob or Teddy, a third animation, Cat, appeared. Daniel looked at Cat and then at the therapist and back to Cat. His mother explained that he liked cats. It was a good example of a (genuinely) unexpected event producing an opportunity for the child to communicate in order to redirect the therapist's attention.

Discussion

The previous section outlined four microcomputer-based joint activities and highlighted how each could be used to encourage a child to communicate in order to fulfil a specific function. We gave examples of the sort of software that could be used with each activity. There is a danger in this kind of description that a misleadingly rigid picture is painted, something like:

activity = particular software = child expresses particular function.

In this section we want to illustrate how this apparently rigid approach is, in practice, not as directive as it might sound.

In fact, we would argue that it is not the adult partner, nor the technology, nor the child that has the final say in how this type of intervention unfolds, but the combination of all three. More precisely, the outcome is determined by how the adult partner and the child 'agree' to interpret the meaning of the events generated by the computer.

The same computer-generated sequence of events may be interpreted quite differently on different occasions. For example, a simple piece of software may display a face at the press of a switch. Initially it might be used within the **Attending Together** routine, but later, as the child becomes accustomed to this sequence of events, s/he may start to precede each appearance of the face with a gesture which the adult partner interprets as expressing a request for the face to reappear. Although the same software has been used throughout, the tone of the activity has developed and is more accurately described by the **Make it Change!** activity.

The shared nature of action and interpretation

The 'jointness' of a joint activity is dependent on both adult partner and child interpreting the events that occur in a similar way. And both the adult partner and the child have a part to play in influencing the way this happens. In the example above we saw how the child can take the initiative, as the situation is reinterpreted to allow him or her a more active role in 'demanding' the reappearance of an image. In this case the adult partner might acknowledge the subtle reinterpretation that has taken place by combining gestures, facial expression and intonation to formulate a question such as 'Do you want to see the face?'. On another occasion the child might seemingly take the initiative in order to bring an activity to a close – maybe turning away in his or her chair. The adult partner can then interpret this body movement as a sign of refusal, and the session could be brought to an end with a comment like 'So you've had enough then!'.

Indeed with children who are learning to communicate, the adult partner's interpretation of their actions has a basic importance. Initially a child may be unaware that his or her actions can affect the way others behave, and it is only because the adult partner responds in a consistent way to particular gestures, movements and vocalizations that the child learns s/he can (intentionally) communicate with others (Goldbart, 1988b).

Of course the adult partner also has the potential to initiate changes in the way an activity is defined. S/he can select software that is more likely to lead to one type of activity than another. For example, single event software is more likely to lead to an **Attending Together** than it is to a **Pretend Friend** activity. And, at a more subtle level, the adult may introduce 'unexpected events' (McClenny et al, 1992). This may involve delaying the press of a switch, or looking the other way, so that the child is provoked into communicating in a new kind of way. For these unexpected events to be successful, both child and adult must share an understanding of what they mean. A delay in pressing the switch may result, for instance, in a cartoon character not making his normal appearance, with the shared meaning one of 'surprise' ('Where is he?'). Alternatively, by looking away the adult partner may be conveying the impression that his attention has been distracted, and needs to be redirected back to the screen by the child.

Constrained choice and shared meaning

It would seem, then, that one of the most important features of software-based joint action routines is that they provide situations that are constrained, while allowing some scope for choice and flexibility in the meaning of what happens next. There is a limit to the number of ways in which the actions of either the adult partner or child may be interpreted. For example, a child may act as if to 'demand' the next step in a sequence of images; point to something on the screen that s/he wishes the adult to attend to; or give indications that s/he has had enough of the activity and wishes to do something else. Similarly in the simplified context of the joint activity it is easier for the child to make sense of the adult's behaviour and for the two of them to reach a shared interpretation of its meaning.

Although in the previous section joint activities were presented as a list of single and discrete entities from which the adult partner selects, once the activity begins the situation is likely to be much more fluid. In practice activities mutate and evolve into one another, restart and terminate, according to the shared interpretation of actions that stem from both the adult partner and the child.

CHAPTER 3

Developing information technology competencies

Tina Detheridge

Introduction

There are pupils with severe multiple disabilities who do not have easily interpretable means of communicating ideas. Their understanding and capabilities are hard to identify through currently validated assessment tools. The two most common types of assessment are those that rely on observing responses to particular behaviour tasks, and open systems (based on Piaget's cognitive development theories) that provide a framework for more general observation. Glenn and O'Brien (1994) provide an overview of these approaches. The behaviourist model is concerned with responses to events or stimuli; the cognitive development model is concerned with identifying underlying understanding. However, assessment tools currently available for either approach, whilst providing frameworks for observing current achievement, provide little guidance on potential or hidden capability. They do not, in the main, provide a structure for progression – in other words, they help to identify where a student is 'at', but not where a student should 'go'.

Information technology can provide mechanisms for allowing students with severe disabilities to demonstrate capability. A structured series of stimuli and activities can be used for observational assessment as well as suggesting steps of progression.

Background

Information Technology (IT) has been widely used with pupils with severe learning difficulties and those with physical disabilities for many years, with considerable success. It has provided unique and powerful opportunities for communication and access to learning. The use of IT with pupils with severe multiple disabilities has had a rather less dramatic impact. One reason may be the difficulties in identifying appropriate learning objectives and in recognising steps of progression that can be achieved through IT activities. In social programmes the objectives are clearer, being mainly to develop interactive skills that contribute towards communication. There are some pupils, however, whose physical disabilities are so severe that they are unable to demonstrate what they may understand, and whose communication mechanisms are so underdeveloped that their cognitive capabilities remain unassessed.

David was fifteen and had been in his new school for about nine months when I met him. David was almost permanently in spasm, he had no recognisable communication skills – neither a 'yes' nor a 'no' equivalent. Although he took a great delight in human contact he had not developed a means of interacting other than on a broad response basis. His teacher, however, noted that David would sometimes laugh. She felt sure that this was a laugh and not a facial spasm and that it was voluntary, being in response to some event that he recognized.

Ben, who is eight, has clear 'yes' and 'no' gestures, but no speech. He has just started to use a communication aid with a small number of symbols attached to a set of sentences concerning home/school activities. He clearly understands quite a lot of the events around him, but as yet has no mechanism of responding other than with his yes/no. He has no tools for exploring ideas, developing basic cognitive awareness of shape and sequence etc., or of putting ideas together to make self-initiated communication expressions.

Pupils like David may be able to learn to use a switch to operate a computer or a communication device. Using these tools he may be able to express preferences, to participate in social interactions, and to develop new concepts and skills. Ben, given a means of using a computer, could learn to write using symbols or pictures, to match, sort and sequence shapes, numbers and ideas, and eventually to develop basic literacy and numeracy skills and to participate in a broad curriculum.

Both these pupils will require a complex range of communication skills to maximize their potential both as school pupils and in their adult lives. For many pupils like David and Ben, computer-based technology is going to provide an essential component in their armoury of tools. For this reason it is vital that they develop IT skills.

There are many computer controlled aids that may be used. These include communication aids, sensory environments and speech output devices. Other electrically controlled equipment such as toys, fans or tape recorders may also be adapted to operate through switches (see Watts; Reed and Addis, this volume). For the purpose of this chapter the discussion is mainly confined to computer activities, although it is intended that these may be generalized and the skills applied in other contexts.

Assessment

Any programme of learning must be tailored to the needs and capabilities of the individual. Assessment of current capability is, therefore, an important prerequisite to programme planning. However, there are difficulties in assessing pupils with multiple disabilities. A review of the literature on assessment techniques and protocols reveals that there are few tools available suitable for this group. For example, test batteries such as the Behavioural Assessment Battery (Kiernan and Jones, 1982) prescribe a pre-defined set of skills to be assessed. These tests rely on the pupil being able to make clear, unambiguous responses. On the other hand open frameworks such as the Affective Communication Assessment (Coupe et al., 1985), which allow the assessor to set the criteria, do not provide a clear set of skills and capabilities against which to measure the achievement of the individual.

For many teachers and carers an intuitive understanding of the individual in their social context may be adequate for determining a set of social objectives. However, such intuitive observation can lack rigour, and may be difficult to use to convince others. How many times have we worked with an individual when we have been absolutely sure that there is genuine interaction, and that he or she is aware of the communication, but have nevertheless been unable to demonstrate this to others? IT can provide a reliable and reproducible stimulus, against which individual responses can be observed. Although much of the interaction will involve a teacher or carer, the independent stimulus will help to provide a mechanism for unambiguous and objective assessment. The success will depend upon having appropriate conditions and IT resources for the process.

Sanjit's case provides an example of the types of area where IT may lead to a more detailed and objective assessment of a student. Sanjit enjoys the company of his school friends and being included in all classroom activities. He cannot actively join in, and relies on the general feeling of inclusion for his enjoyment. He seems to respond to some friends more than others, which suggests that he is capable of discrimination. One objective that his teacher would like to achieve is to find a way in which he could do something on his own.

Sanjit was given a switch linked to a picture building program. Initially he pressed the switch in a rather uncontrolled rapid fashion, but when it was placed so that he had to reach out to it, his action became more purposeful. He seemed to realize very quickly that there was some link between pressing this switch and the appearance of picture and sound on the screen. The evidence for this was that he would look at the screen quite often, until the picture set was complete. When no further pictures appeared he stopped pressing the switch. The program was reset and he started to press the switch again. This demonstration was repeated several times. From this clearer, more objective evidence we could gather that Sanjit could pay attention to an image on a computer screen. He could also press a switch and understand that this action was linked in some way to the screen. IT offered the first demonstration that Sanjit had understanding of any precise action or effect. This allowed Sanjit's teachers to assess certain capabilities, and to infer other skills that might be stimulated.

Julie showed interest in her surroundings, turning her head to look at people and actions in the room, but she had no formal communication. She would smile or frown but this was not sufficiently developed to provide a reliable means of communication. After a great deal of trial and error, over many weeks, a switch and position was found that Julie managed to press reliably. As soon as she had this switch, connected to picture building activities, she showed a great interest in the computer, with animated responses to each new picture. She would build a picture three or four times until she was sure of it and would then become bored, refusing to carry on. As soon as a new picture was presented she would start again. From this we inferred that she could discriminate between pictures and understood the sequence of the picture building activity.

Both these students used IT to demonstrate hidden competencies, but the identification was a casual and rather ad hoc process. What is necessary is a structured sequence of skills against which each pupil may be assessed as part of a detailed observation of their individual capabilities, and we discuss this below.

Identifying competencies

A checklist developed by Jo Douglas at Great Ormond Street Hospital in 1986 (see Detheridge and Hopkins, 1991) provides a useful aid to assessing a child's ability to use a computer, and has provided the basis of an hierarchy of skills that may be used as an assessment framework. The Douglas checklist identifies a series of steps of progression in four areas: visual attention to the screen, motivation, concentration and physical control. These areas have been found to be interdependent, and it has proved difficult to assess each area independently. Although the cognitive development of the individual is implicit in the scales, it has been found in practice that an integrated approach, with more overt recognition of cognition, is more useful. This approach is detailed in the next section.

Skills for developing IT capability as a prerequisite for using IT to develop communication, cognition and attention

Awareness

This includes visual and auditory awareness. A series of finely graded stimuli is required for the teacher to observe responses. Assessment is based on responses that are repeated a number of times. There is no requirement for the pupil to use an input or controlling device or switch at this stage.

- Is the individual aware of the computer screen?
- Does s/he show any animated response to certain images and/or sounds?
- What is the level of stimulus needed? e.g. size and contrast of image, sound reinforcement, animation or static image.
- Will s/he respond to images with and without sound reinforcement?
- Is there need for a human prompt (speech, touching the screen etc.)?
- Can s/he track a large image moving over the screen (e.g. Figure 3.1)?

Figure 3.1: Using animated software to assist in observing children's responses to images

- Can s/he follow a series of actions and show some interest in the changes?
- Is there any sense of anticipation shown after a predictable sequence of actions?

Interaction

This set of skills concerns pupil interaction with a computer, use of a switch and understanding the relationship between cause-and-effect. It is difficult to separate the physical components of interaction from the cognitive and social. The social (teacher) and computer (visual or sound) rewards will encourage the development of the physical skills which in turn will stimulate cognitive development. For this reason no attempt is made to isolate each separate skill at these early stages of interaction.

- Can the pupil use a switch? (Is there a known reliable physical movement, and can a suitable switch be placed for easy use)?
- Can s/he hit the switch without searching for it each time?
- Can s/he hit the switch whilst looking at the computer screen?
- Does s/he appear to understand that there is some kind of relationship between hitting the switch and the screen actions (sound and image)?
- Can s/he understand and sustain interaction to complete a short sequence, such as building a picture?
- Will s/he anticipate a part of the process – for example by smiling or vocalising just before a tune is played?
- Are there signs of enjoyment and achievement at the interaction between screen and pupil, both with and without adult intervention?
- Will s/he stop pressing the switch if no screen response is achieved? (e.g. at the end of a sequence?)
- Can s/he recognize different images?

Control

To refine the level of interaction between the pupil and computer activity, a level of physical control and understanding is required. The next stage, therefore, is to develop an understanding of the nature of the relationship between the switch and the computer actions, and to establish a one-to-one correspondence between each physical movement of the switch and the effect on the screen.

- Will the pupil press the switch in relation to the screen activity – e.g. on a picture building activity, will s/he stop pressing when the picture is complete?
- Can s/he press a switch at just the right time to make the effect?
- Can s/he avoid pressing the switch at the wrong time?
- Can s/he understand that there are effective and non-effective times to press the switch?
- Can s/he shift attention from one area of the screen to another?

- Can s/he move attention from one object to another?
- Can s/he press a switch at a reasonably precise time, or in relation to a precise event, to achieve a predictable response?

Choosing

The final area of capability necessary for using a computer effectively as a learning and communication tool is to use it to select, indicate or make choices. The methods used may depend upon the physical capabilities and input devices that the pupil can use. For example, when making selections there are two actions necessary – one to point to or move an indicating device to a required item on the screen, and one positively to make the selection. Pupils who can use two or more switches will be able to use one switch for each action. A single switch user will need to develop the skills required to use an automatically moving indicator.

In Figure 3.2, the box around the pictures moves from one item to another. The pupil presses the switch when it is around the item that s/he wants to select. The box cursor changes colour to show that a selection has been made.

Figure 3.2: Communicating choices by selecting images on the computer screen

This selection process is very complex, requiring both physical control and understanding of the process. It may be helpful in the initial stages to break this selection process down into smaller steps. For example, a single switch user may find difficulty in learning to control an automatically moving pointer, although s/he can understand the concept and make the choice itself. The teacher may assist this by moving the indicating pointer in response to the attention and understanding of the pupil, but leaving time for the pupil to make a selection when s/he wishes.

The important purpose, of the pupil making and indicating a choice, can in this way be achieved through cooperation.

Once this skill has been mastered there is a vast array of activities that can support communication and learning. In these instances IT helps the pupil to communicate understanding. It can also enable pupils with severe physical limitations to explore and manipulate concepts such as sorting, matching and sequencing, when they are unable to handle concrete objects or to sign effectively.

Work plans and progression

Moving on from assessment

Many of the capabilities discussed above may be developed in a variety of ways, depending on the skills and interests of the individual. The list of capabilities may, as discussed, provide a useful starting point to the initial assessment of pupils who will be using IT as part of their educational programmes. A clear picture of the pupil's current capabilities is an essential prerequisite to planning any programme of work. The teacher's personal knowledge and observation of the pupil will identify an approximate level of capability, which can then be developed and substantiated by careful and detailed observation.

The most important element in using IT as a communication and learning tool is the pupil's mechanism of control. Assessment of a pupil's ability will depend on their having an appropriate mechanism of interacting with a computer (referred to here as a switch); it is also necessary that s/he is seated in an appropriate manner to facilitate ease of switch use; that s/he can see the computer screen easily and comfortably, and that s/he has adequate opportunity to develop and practise the necessary skills of computer interaction (Detheridge, 1995).

The area that causes the greatest difficulty is providing a good, reliable input mechanism (see also Reed and Addis, this volume). This is, however, an absolutely essential prerequisite to effective IT use. A switch needs to be fixed firmly in the same position for each occasion. The pupil must be able to activate a switch without undue effort. If lifting a hand is difficult then a soft arm rest may be useful. If the pupil has a tendency to press the switch continuously in an aimless fashion, then putting the switch at a distance where s/he must reach for it may help. If a touchscreen is to be used, care must be taken so that lifting the hand is not tiring, and that the hand will not obscure the image at a crucial moment. If a lever or press switch is used the pupil will need to be able to release the switch as easily as pressing it. A switch mounted onto a block so that a sideways hand movement activates it may be more useful than a lifting action in some cases.

A pupil with learning difficulties may need a constant type of switch use. S/he may become confused if sometimes the switch action varies from task to task. For example, most computer programs require discrete press and release action for each step of the activity, whereas other devices such as tape recorders, toys and lights operate only when a switch is held closed. This problem can be overcome by using a latching timer to the toy activity so that it also operates on a discrete press action. The timer then will give a preset period of action from the toy, and another switch press is required for it to continue.

For both Sanjit and Julie, the first and most important task was to find a reliable switch action, and to be able to set the switch up in a constant position. Julie's lower jaw movement was her most reliable physical action, and so a small switch was mounted on an armature that could be fixed to her tray. Sanjit used a large switch so that his hand position was not critical. Both pupils were carefully seated so that they could see the screen at an optimum distance without any reflections. The assessments and subsequent practice sessions took place in a quiet, reasonably distraction-free environment. On each occasion a wide range of computer programs was available so that the teacher could select new images or activities according to the pupil responses. These preconditions are essential before attempting to embark on either an assessment or a programme of work. Establishing the preconditions and the assessment should ideally involve all the professionals working with the pupil. The speech and language and occupational therapists will each make a valuable contribution to choosing the optimum solution.

Aims and objectives

The purposes of using a computer as part of a communication and learning programme are part of the overall educational aims for that pupil. The computer is a mechanism for attaining those aims. Attached to each aim will be a set of discrete objectives which may be closely identified with one particular strategy. So, for example the educational aim for David was to develop a means of communicating requests. The objectives were to find a mechanism by which he could indicate a response, whether gestural or electronic, and to develop his capability to understand and make choices. These objectives were broken down into a series of small steps, each of which described an activity designed to contribute towards reaching this objective. David's steps included using switch-operated program to develop understanding of cause-and-effect, develop a reliable method of controlling a single switch, and experiencing a variety of different uses and contexts in which he could exercise control. The second set of steps introduced recognition of images and photographs to represent objects and actions, such as a photograph of chocolate, a computer drawing of drink, so that he might learn to use these representations to indicate choices. Accompanying this, David was to be given a range of situations in which he could regularly make genuine choices.

Although the computer played a large part in the development of these skills, all the staff were encouraged to generalize the activities. David was encouraged to use his new found confidence to express pleasure and disapproval through facial gestures, to understand that these expressions conveyed meaning. A particularly important and difficult area arose in giving choices. *Making decisions and giving genuine choices to someone who has learned passivity is a lengthy process.* It is also inconvenient in a busy classroom. There is a temptation to pretend to give choices, or only to give occasional opportunities – neither of which are much use to the struggling pupil.

Programmes of work

Ben

Aims:

Ben is already learning to understand quite a wide vocabulary. He needs to be able to manage an input device reliably so that he can make selections on a screen, to make phrases, sequence numbers and to develop pre-writing activities. Eventually, it is hoped, he will become a reader and writer, using IT to overcome his physical disabilities.

Short term objectives:

Ben can see a screen easily, enjoys different images and effects and clearly shows preferences. He understands that his switch presses are related to the screen activity, but does not yet understand quite in what way. Ben needs programs that help him develop one-to-one correspondence between switch press and immediate screen response, and he will then be able to show understanding by responding to simple requests. Ben is working towards mastery of control skills.

Immediate IT activity:

The first step is to use a program that will produce a result for each press but will not allow inappropriate presses. This will be followed by games such as snap where he is to press at the right time to make a choice or to complete a symbol phrase such as 'I like.'

Sanjit

Aims:

Sanjit would enjoy a wider range of activities in which he could take a really active part. Some computer activities can be played by more than one person and he may develop a sense of companionship by sharing an activity with a friend.

Short term objectives:

Sanjit will learn to use a switch to be able to control a computer-based activity. If he succeeds in managing a switch and understands the cause-and-effect he may apply this skill to other devices such as a tape recorder.

The next objective will be to establish whether Sanjit has preferences and can show them, such as favourite television programmes, favourite music. At present his lack of ability to control or communicate prevents him projecting opinions. Sanjit is working towards attaining interaction skills.

Immediate steps:

The first step is to make sure that Sanjit really understands that it is he who is creating the picture on the screen. As well as encouraging control skills, his teachers will help him to concentrate and develop a sense of anticipation. For this he will use a fairly small set of activities, although each has a reasonable range of different images to add variety. One limiting factor is the small range of activities with images that are appropriate to a 16 year old young man.

Julie

Aims:

Julie certainly shows an interest in her surroundings. At present she does not appear to understand much language, although she seems to enjoy sounds and music. The aim is to help her to make choices and express opinions.

Short term objectives:

Evidence suggests that Julie would like to be able to play by herself sometimes rather than always being dependent upon an adult. The first objective is to find a mechanism whereby she can control a switch and use a range of stimulating computer activities on her own as well as with support and encouragement from an adult. Julie is working simultaneously on developing control skills and acquiring interaction skills.

Immediate steps:

Julie will use programs where she can build pictures, change pictures or follow simple animated stories or sequences. This will help her to understand some of the ways that she could play on her own, as well as developing interactive skills. She will need a variety of images and effects, and her teacher will look out for signs of preference, likes and dislikes.

Naomi

Aims:

When Naomi first started school a year ago she would cry any time she was left without physical contact with an adult. She has settled into school well but is still very dependent upon other people. Her teacher would like her to be able to sustain an independent activity for short periods of time.

Short term objectives:

Naomi has a small number of battery-operated toys that she enjoys in company with her teacher, but these rely on a fair amount of physical intervention – keeping the toy in view, and providing a lot of vocal feedback. Naomi will be encouraged to use a range of computer-based activities to develop other interests and to start to play games herself, with the computer providing feedback as an alternative to the adult. Naomi is working towards developing attention skills and higher levels of interaction.

Immediate steps:

The first task for Naomi is to develop a clear understanding that she is causing the screen activities, and to relate this to other communication work. Her teacher is using screen prints of the characters and encouraging her to look at the picture of each screen character as she calls it up. She enjoys this very much and already gets pleasure from the activity itself and is less dependent upon human company. She will play with Blob and other screen characters for short periods, and gains obvious enjoyment from some of the activities. Her computer 'corner' is a very lively focal point of the classroom, and she is often the star.

Recording achievement

Each one of these pupils has long term goals that will benefit their whole learning situation. Each is embarking upon distinct, achievable tasks that they can practise daily with the support of a teacher or carer. Screen prints, photographs, regular notes of each activity and the corresponding responses contribute to a real sense of achievement with each of these pupils.

One of the most important aspects of recording outcomes is the opportunity to see when things are not working as well, so that the objectives or tasks may be modified. Tangible illustrations will contribute to the regular records of achievement, as well as forming the basis for regular review. Children who make progress in very small steps need as much encouragement and feedback for their efforts as any other child. Teachers, parents and other carers also need encouragement. Clear evidence of the pupil's achievements, however small, shows that the efforts are worthwhile and purposeful and gives everybody confidence in the progress.

CHAPTER 4

The development of early tactile reading skills

Graeme Douglas and Jean Dickens

Introduction

This chapter considers, broadly, the use of technology in the teaching of tactile reading to young children with multiple disabilities and visual impairments. More precisely, it describes an approach using a concept keyboard, tactile overlays, and associated digitized sounds.

The chapter focuses upon the interaction between teacher, child and computer. It is argued that both teacher and computer support, or 'scaffold', the child's reading, and that the teacher has the vital role of changing the degree of scaffolding provided according to the needs of the child. The learning activity is designed so that the computer is able to take some of the burden of providing information, freeing the teacher to interact more flexibly with the child.

The learning activity – contingent teaching

A number of studies have explored the ways in which an adult 'teacher' can scaffold a child's performance on a learning activity (e.g. Wood et al., 1976; Wood et al., 1978). These studies have focused on the completion of non-technological tasks, for example building a pyramid from interlocking wooden blocks (similar to a jigsaw puzzle). A common factor is that the child cannot complete the task alone, but relies upon the help of the teacher.

Wood et al. (1978) note various different types or levels of instruction given by teacher to child:

- Level 1 – general verbal encouragement.
- Level 2 – specific verbal instruction.

- Level 3 – assists in choice of material.
- Level 4 – prepares material for assembly.
- Level 5 – demonstrates an operation.

For the purpose of illustration, we will consider these categories of instruction more precisely, using the familiar example of an adult and child constructing a jigsaw together.

At the first level, the adult may offer simple verbal encouragement, for example: 'Try and do the jigsaw.' At the next level, the verbal instruction is more precise, for instance: 'Try and find a blue piece.' At level 3, the adult may point to two pieces which are approximately the right shape and colour, and say 'Try one of those blue ones.' At level 4, the adult may find an appropriate piece of jigsaw, and position it so that the child can more easily push the piece 'home'. Finally, at level 5, the adult may demonstrate how two pieces of jigsaw fit together, in other words, show the child.

Wood (1988) points out that as the adult moves down the list, the specificity of the instruction *increases,* while the degree of responsibility the child bears for how to proceed in the task *decreases*. Another, attractive way of conceptualizing the list is that as the level of instruction increases, the teacher *scaffolds* the child in succeeding at the task to a greater degree.

Importantly, the success of the instruction appears to rely upon the way these levels of scaffolding are combined – the instruction should be *contingent* upon the child's needs. An adult teacher might be asked to combine 'telling' and showing' as follows:

> When a child makes an error, then immediately take over more control. So, for example, if an error occurs in response to a level three intervention, advance to level 4 or 5. However, if the child is successful in following an instruction (for example, level 3) relinquish some control. That is, next time an error or pause invites an instruction, intervene at levels 1 or 2.
>
> (Wood, 1980, p.286)

This relies upon the skill of the tutor of course – and this skill should not be underestimated. However, it also relies upon the flexibility of the activity. The activity must 'afford' these different types of interactions. If the activity affords only showing, or only telling, then it is unlikely to succeed. In this chapter we concentrate upon the use of computers in designing and implementing learning activities. The examples described have the flexibility which allows contingent teaching to take place.

Modification for children with sensory disabilities

Wood and his co-workers have used this approach in working with profoundly deaf children (e.g. Wood, 1980; Wood, 1989). They have tried to transfer the scaffolding description of tutoring used in studies with hearing children. Using the definitions given above, the degree of contingent teaching was compared to the success with which the deaf children learnt a task. On first analysis, tutorial contingency and the children's performance bore no relationship. The reason for this was that the initial analysis included some solely verbal instructions, in that levels 1 and 2 were defined in exclusively verbal terms. In practice, the teacher usually complemented a verbal instruction with a nonverbal one, and when this was accounted for, the relationship was re-established.

On first reading, discussion of deaf children might seem irrelevant in a chapter concerned with blind children. However, the points made by Wood can be transferred to our context, raising the question whether visual disability has any implications for the scaffolding a tutor must provide for a child. The answer, of course, is yes.

Naturally, it is important that scaffolding provided for blind children is non-visual. The precise nature of this scaffolding will be discussed in the light of the skills being taught, and observation of a teacher and children, later in this chapter.

The computer as an instructional medium

Blenkhorn (1986) has summarized how information flows between computer and user (whether visually impaired or otherwise) via input and output devices. It is essential that the methods of input and output are suitable for the user, and Blenkhorn argues that the particular qualities of some devices make the computer a potentially useful educational tool for children with visual impairments. For example, input devices such as switches and keyboards, and output devices such as speech synthesizers and backlit monitors with high contrasting colours, provide access to information for a broad range of people of various ages and abilities, and with varying visual impairments (see Tobin, this volume).

Just as the scaffolding provided by the teacher must take account of the learner's needs, so the computer output must also be of an appropriate type if computers are to be used in the scaffolding process. In this chapter, the output modality we are concerned with is *digitized sound*.

Digitized sounds are essentially natural sounds which can be captured by, and stored upon, a computer (as natural sounds can be captured by a tape recorder). With appropriate software (in this case Centre

SoundBook; RCEVH, 1993, 1994) they can be replayed through the computer's sound system at any time. The true advantage of digitized sounds is that they sound natural and 'real', and thus can be more easily interpreted by the listener.

The scaffolding process not only demands the presentation of information of the appropriate type, but also that it be presented at the appropriate time. If the child is to act in a way which the computer can respond to, an input device appropriate for the child in question must be provided

The concept keyboard is an input device which consists of a flat 'tray' of (at least) 128 buttons or areas. It can be programmed so that when particular areas of the keyboard are pressed, prerecorded digitized sounds are heard. As described, software exists to record any sound, and associate this sound with any area of the concept keyboard.

Importantly, tactile 'overlays' appropriate for blind children can be placed on top of the concept keyboard. The overlay can provide a 'key' for the blind child indicating where to press (and where not to press). Similar arrangements have been used to create talking tactile maps for older and more able blind people, and to provide 'auditory pictures' for young braille readers (see Bozic and McCall, 1993; Douglas and Greaney, 1995). The arrangement is summarized in Figure 4.1.

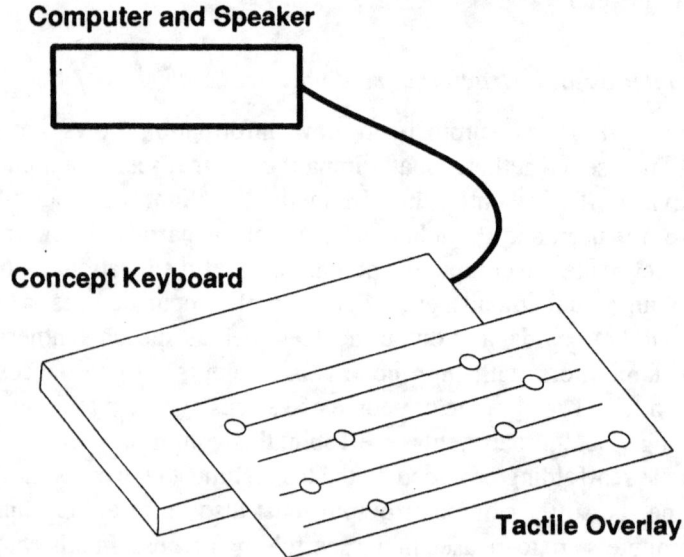

Figure 4.1: Diagram of a computer connected to a concept keyboard with an overlay

Teaching Moon reading skills

The discussion so far has described the theoretical approach of this chapter, together with an outline of some useful computer equipment. The following sections are intended to bring these two themes together with a concrete example: the imaginative use of a computer and concept keyboard for teaching Moon reading skills. Moon is a simplified, raised line version of the Roman print alphabet (see Figure 4.2).

∧ a	∪ b	⊂ c	⊃ d	⌈ e	⌐ f	⌉ g	o h	⎮ i	⌡ j
< k	∟ l	⌐ m	N n	O o	∠ p	⌐ q	\ r	/ s	⎯ t
		∪ u	∨ v	∩ w	> x	⌡ y	Z z		

Figure 4.2: The Moon Alphabet

The embossed characters of the code provide a clear outline with distinct shapes, making Moon a seemingly more appropriate medium for those with less sensitive touch (McCall et al., 1994).

Broad aims and existing methods of teaching

The children involved in this case study are three educationally blind children with severe learning difficulties ('Educationally blind' is the term used to describe those unable to read print, who require tactile reading methods). The first child was ten years old when the study was carried out. She appears to have no light perception in either eye due to retinopathy of prematurity. The second child was eight years old, and appears to be totally blind due to bilateral optic nerve hypoplasia. The third child was eleven years old when this study was carried out. She is anopthalmic (born without eyes). Moon had been adopted as a route to literacy for these children, and had been introduced during the previous year. As well as the computer with concept keyboard, a number of resources were used for this purpose (see McCall et al., 1994):

- Reading materials with 'Moon characters' (e.g. Mot and Tot the cats) with supporting audio tapes.
- Moon books (these and the above evolved into a teaching pack: see McCall et al., 1995).
- The use of Moon labels (e.g. on the children's drawers).
- A 'swish' card machine and materials.

So what was the motivation to include another medium for teaching Moon? Why was the use of a concept keyboard considered? The following general areas were identified:

1. As an alternative approach, to provide interest and motivation. This was to prove additionally important because of the slow progress made by the children – the variety of activities was important to maintain the children's motivation (as well as the teacher's!).
2. The concept keyboard could provide easier and more rapid feedback to the children than other media available.
3. Related to (2), there was the need for an activity that could be managed relatively easily by the teacher. For example, children's attention could be easily lost from the task in hand while the teacher operated a tape recorder.

Sample activities

A distinction can be made between a 'sound node' (a tactile area that if pressed will make a noise), a 'tactile node' (a tactile area which conveys information but does not have an associated sound, e.g. a Moon character), and a 'tactile path' (a tactile strip which connects nodes). Using these terms for reference, the following section describes two of the activities.

Tracking – Listening to chunks of a story

This overlay (see Figure 4.3) involves the attachment of chunks of a story (adapted from *Peace at Last* by Jill Murphy, Macmillan Children's Books) to each node. The story described continues over two 'sweeps' of the overlay. After the first sweep, the teacher loads the second set of sound associations into the computer and the child 'reads' the second half of the story. This might be likened to turning a page.

Only the first half of the story is given here. A tactile path on the overlay connects sound nodes and as each sound node is pressed, the computer 'speaks' a chunk of the story. Working from top left along the tactual lines through each node, the child 'reads' the following chunks of story:

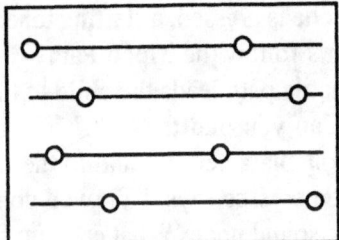

Figure 4.3: The tracking overlay (listening to chunks of a story)

- The hour was late.
- Mr Bear was tired. Mrs Bear was tired. And Baby Bear was tired. So they all went to bed.
- Mrs Bear fell asleep. Mr Bear didn't.
- Mrs Bear began to snore. [Snore] said Mrs Bear. [Snore, Snore]
- 'Oh no!' said Mr Bear, 'I can't stand this.' So he got up and went to sleep in Baby Bear's room.
- Baby Bear wasn't asleep either. He was lying in bed pretending to be an aeroplane. [Neoow] said Baby Bear. [Neoow] [Neoow]. 'Oh no!' said Mr Bear, 'I can't stand this.' So he got up and went to sleep in the living room.
- Tick tock went the living room clock. Tick tock, tick tock [sound of a cuckoo clock]. 'Oh no!' said Mr Bear, 'I can't stand this.' So he got up and went to sleep in the kitchen.
- Drip drip went the kitchen tap. Mmmmm went the refrigerator. 'Oh no!' said Mr Bear, 'I can't stand this.' So he got up and went to sleep in the garden.

Phonics – Deriving phonemes from letters:

This overlay (see Figure 4.4) involves the attachment of relevant phonemes to Moon characters (here 'T' and 'M'). A description of the overlay is given below, starting from the top left sound node and moving along the path as if reading.

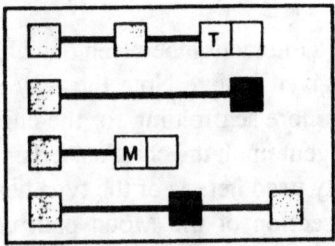

Figure 4.4: Following the Moon Path overlay (phonemes 'T' and 'M')

When the first sound node is pressed, a starting tune is played followed by a verbal message: 'Let's follow the Moon Path – I wonder what we will find.' Following the tactile path leads the child to the second node which speaks the message 'Can you find the "T"?' The path leads to a tactile node which is the Moon character 'T', and to the right of this is another sound node which when pressed says '"T", well done.' Moving along the tactile path leads to the sound node 'What can you find on the Moon path beginning with "T"?', and the next node is a piece of towel which when pressed says 'A towel, well done!' and plays a musical tune.

Similarly, the next sound node asks 'Can you find the "M"?' The path leads to a tactile node which is the Moon character 'M', and to the right of this is another sound node which when pressed says '"M", well done.' Moving along the tactile path leads to the sound node 'What can you find on the Moon path beginning with "M"?', and the next node is a piece of mat which when pressed says 'A mat, well done!' and plays a musical tune. The final node says 'That's the end of the Moon path', and plays another tune.

A number of overlays were developed with this format. The beginning and end of the task were signalled by tunes which were consistent. The whole task could be thought of as consisting of sub-tasks, each signalled by questions such as finding a letter, or something beginning with a letter.

Observing the activities

The following section seeks to describe and summarize some of the observations made of teacher and child interactions during the computer-assisted activity. The interactions were video taped for ease of analysis. The presentation of the observations reflects the theoretical standpoint described in the introduction – evidence is presented of contingent tutoring, and examples of how the computer-based activities provide opportunities for these interactions.

Examples of dialogues

Two separate extracts of interaction between one child and the teacher in the same activity are given below. Note the way in which the teacher progressively provides more scaffolding for the child, and how the level of scaffolding is contingent upon the child's needs.

The computer activity used here is of the type described in the second example above. This section of the Moon path consists of the Moon character 'T', followed by a sound node, 'Can you find something beginning with "T"?' Following the tactile path leads to another sound node, which when pressed plays the sound of a turkey. The 'rules' of the activity are such that the child is required to say what the sound is.

Computer: [Computer sound of a turkey]
Teacher: What's that one? You've heard that already this morning.
[Pause]
Teacher: Do you remember? [takes the child's hand back along the path to the relevant part]
[Pause]
Teacher: What is it? Something beginning with 'T'. Listen.
Computer: [Computer sound of a turkey] (teacher presses).
Teacher: It's a turkey, Gerry.
Child: Turkey.

The scaffolding provided by the teacher is increased until she finally provides the answer. Compare this to the following similar example, where scaffolding of a single level only is required:

Computer: [Sound of running water]
Teacher: What's that? [takes the child's hand back along the path to the relevant part]
Child: It's a tap.

While the contrasts of these interactions appear obvious, it is worth considering the prompts provided by the teacher and computer more carefully. How do they fit with the model presented earlier in the chapter?

Affording scaffolding opportunities

Consider the first interaction presented, and its context. Firstly, the sound is played by the computer (initiated by the child). When the child does not name the sound, the teacher stops the child continuing, and asks the child to name the sound. As the child is clearly struggling to respond, the teacher provides more information to help (reminding her of the criterion that the word must begin with 'T', and replaying the sound). Finally, the teacher provides the answer, the child repeats it, and the activity continues.

Of paramount importance here is that the computer-based activity allows the interactions to occur. For example, the computer provides the sound of a turkey, leaving the child to work out what the sound is. If the child does not name the sound spontaneously, the teacher will prompt, and increase the level of help needed until the child arrives at the correct answer.

If the activity had been designed differently – for instance, if there had been simply the recorded voice 'T is for turkey', then the interaction would not have been able to take place.

Consider the following interaction. This section of the Moon path consists of the Moon character 'T', followed by a sound node, 'Can you find something beginning with "T"?' Following the tactile path leads to a piece of towel, which when pressed plays the message 'A towel, well done!' followed by a musical tune.

> *Computer*: Can you find something beginning with 'T'?
> *Teacher*: Follow along the path. [nudges child's hand to the right]
> [The child's hand wanders off the path, and the teacher moves the hand back on to where the path was left.]
> *Teacher*: Gerry, come on. [nudges child's hand to the right]
> [The child moves along the path and finds the towel.]
> *Teacher*: What have you found? [prevents the child pressing]
> *Child*: 'T'.
> *Teacher*: Something beginning with 'T'.
> *Child*: A towel. [teacher lets child press switch]
> *Computer*: A towel, well done. [tune].

On first inspection, the material appears to contradict the point raised above – the computer simply tells the child the answer ('A towel...'). However, notice how the teacher manages the activity in such a way as to prompt an interaction between herself and the child.

How does the activity fit with the categories of instruction proposed by Wood? Firstly, as a reminder, Wood's categories are listed below (remember these are for instructions given by a tutor in a block construction exercise similar to a jigsaw):

- Level 1 – general verbal encouragement.
- Level 2 – specific verbal instruction.
- Level 3 – assists in choice of material.
- Level 4 – prepares material for assembly.
- Level 5 – demonstrates an operation.

Just as Wood (1980) had difficulty in categorizing interactions between teachers and deaf children, the process is similarly problematic here. Firstly, nonverbal strategies such as pointing and showing are problematic because the children cannot see. Secondly, detailed verbal descriptions are also inappropriate because the language is too advanced for the children's needs.

Physical scaffolding

Discussion to date has concentrated upon the verbal interaction between teacher, computer, and child. However, the teacher also intervened physically. This has similarities to what Wood would call 'showing' the child what to do, but this description is too simple for these interactions. The physical interventions can be categorized as serving one of two functions, both means of scaffolding the child's learning:

- To show or demonstrate.
- To restrict.

The first function is the more obvious one. The teacher shows or demonstrates what the child should be doing – for example pressing firmly upon sound areas, moving lightly from left to right on the Moon Path, inspecting a Moon character with a light touch, or moving diagonally back from the end of one line to the beginning of the next. In terms of Wood's levels of instruction this is most like Level 5 (demonstration). Their visual disabilities meant that the children could not watch the teacher, and hence, the demonstration required a different mode.

The second function, 'restriction', involves physical intervention by the teacher in a less positive sense. In effect the teacher prevents the child going 'way off beam'. Two examples of this are as follows: firstly, if the child is tracking along a path and wanders off it, the teacher may take the child's hand and move it back onto the path, and then withdraw the help again. This could be likened to what Wood refers to as 'assisting the child in choice of material' (Level 3). The teacher is not telling the child what to do but is implicitly telling the child what not to do.

A further category of teacher intervention was observed, and characterized as 'cupping'. Here the teacher 'cups' the child's hand during parts of the activity, maintaining a readiness to guide (rather akin to stabilizers on a bike). The teacher does not physically withdraw from the child, but maintains a restrictive role. In terms of Wood's levels of instruction this is most like Level 4 – 'preparation of material for assembly' – or positioning the jigsaw piece so the child only has to 'push it home'. It is important to understand the distinction between this restrictive role and a demonstrative one. While the first may be thought of as 'railway tracks', preventing the child going off course, the second is more like an engine, providing the direction and impetus.

A tentative suggestion of the levels of instruction observed here, reflecting the levels suggested by Wood et al. (1976), is presented below, with the agent of the instruction given in brackets:

- Level 1 – general verbal encouragement (teacher and computer).
- Level 2 – specific verbal instruction (teacher and computer).
- Level 3 – correction when 'lost' (teacher).
- Level 4 – restrictive cupping of the child's hand (teacher).
- Level 5 – physical demonstration (teacher).

The problem with the distinctions made above is that when observing the interactions it can be difficult to distinguish physical showing from physical restriction; an observer who does not quiz the teacher might (wrongly) conclude that the teacher is simply dragging the child's hand along the Moon Path. This problem is confounded by the fact that the process is fluid: the teacher subtly changes the type of instruction she provides according to the child's behaviour.

Knowing when to provide which level of scaffolding is a difficult task. However, the activities described here are such that the computer takes 'responsibility' for some aspects of the instruction (the presentation of much of the verbal instruction, and verbal encouragement), allowing the teacher to concentrate upon the needs of the child.

Transference of learning

Transference of learning occurs when the child can use the skills acquired in a different context. It could be argued that this is where the work described in this chapter departs from that of Wood, described earlier. The activity used by Wood (the construction of wooden blocks to form a pyramid) is self-contained. The computer activities were developed in order to help the children learn to read – a somewhat more ambitious aim! However, just as the children in Wood's experiments are building wooden pyramids (albeit with varying amounts of help from the adult tutor), so the children in this study are reading (albeit with help from the teacher and computer). It is hoped that the skills the children learn during these activities will ultimately transfer to a more independent reading activity.

The computer materials present scaffolded instances of reading. In turn, the teacher is responsible for providing the appropriate tutoring for helping the child succeed in these 'reading' tasks. The design of the activity is such that various aspects of reading are permanently scaffolded, as the following examples show:

- The motives for reading are scaffolded by prerecorded prompts, for example:
  - 'Let's follow the moon path . . . '
  - 'Can you find something beginning with "T"?'

- The results of reading are scaffolded by prerecorded sounds, for example:
    - Story elements (chunks of story).
    - Phonic elements (e.g. 'T, well done.')
- The physical process of tracking is scaffolded by the overlay material, for example there are:
    - Clear raised tactile lines to follow.
    - Clear tactile areas containing information.

This unburdens the teacher (and of course the child). The teacher is therefore able to concentrate on providing varying amounts of scaffolding at the level appropriate to the child.

The aim is that interactions between child, computer, and teacher will ultimately become internalized by the child, and he or she will perform these functions alone – for example, s/he will move along the path alone and extract the story without teacher prompting; s/he may be able to read some of the words from Moon in the story without the computer, and so on. As more of these skills become internalized by the child further activities can be developed which assume these skills, and provide opportunities for the teacher to scaffold 'higher' level skills. Evidence for this can be seen in the development of the material. The two activities presented here should not be considered in isolation.

This can be conceptualized as a shift of responsibility from teacher and computer to child for the various parts of the reading activity.

Conclusion

Observation of the activities indicates that they are flexible enough to support a range of needs. Importantly, both the approach the teacher takes and the computer-based material contribute to the flexibility needed.

It is important to emphasize that the activity constitutes more than the computer-based material. All too often, computers are used to teach children prescriptively, with the teacher's role reduced to enforcing the activity. In this study, the contributions of child, teacher and computer were all essential, and their interaction formed the central focus of the activity.

Postscript: the design of activities and overlays

Activity design

All the activities are based around the concept of following a tactile path. The Moon Path is a technique established during the 'Moon as a Route to

Literacy Project' (see Dickens, 1995; McCall etal., 1994). Importantly, an activity involving the Moon Path is intrinsically similar to the basis of tactual reading – tracking over a set of tactual codes from left to right on a page to derive meaning. Activities involving the Moon Path are simple, with rules which children can easily grasp. The path is broken up by a variety of sub-activities, or 'nodes' along the path, which may involve any of the following:

(a) Deriving phonemes from letters.
(b) Combining letters to form a word.
(c) Listening to chunks of a story.
(d) Listening to chunks of music.
(e) Identifying 'objects' (which may be tactual or auditory) beginning with particular phonemes.
(f) Following instructions to do one of the above.

While all the activities share the commonality of following a path, they can be split into two broad categories:

- Tracking.
- Phonics.

In the tracking activities, when the nodes along the path are pressed, pieces of music or story are played (c and d above). In this case, tracking is associated with higher level information. For the phonic activities, nodes along the path involve exercises in phonics, letter identification, or letter combination (a, b, e, and f above). Here, tracking is associated with lower level phonic generation.

Overlay design

A number of strategies are evident in the design of overlays:

1. The material used to construct the overlays is such that it can be distinguished by touch. Further, given materials are consistently used for the same purpose (this is denoted by the different shades of grey used in Figure 4.4). For example felt is used for the first and last instruction 'nodes' (e.g. 'Let's follow the Moon path', 'Can you find . . .', 'That's the end of the Moon path.'), while a metallic material is used beside the Moon characters. Similarly, strips of cork are generally used for the paths between nodes.
2. Auditory information is positioned next to the Moon characters, not beneath them. This is vital because the children should not press firmly on a tactual character, but move over it lightly (see Dickens, 1993).

3. On occasions the path is extended to help guide the child back from the end of one line to the beginning of the next. This guide is interspersed with nodes which play single notes when pressed. Without the guide, this movement frequently needs help from the teacher. The guide proved an alternative method of scaffolding, the child carrying out this movement.
4. Where stories were used, they were designed (or chosen) carefully. Firstly, the stories describe events with which children are likely to be familiar (stories revolve around sounds rather than vision). Secondly, stories have a predictable and repetitive nature allowing the child to become more easily involved in the meaning of the content.

To summarize, the presentation of information is contingent to the child's needs (tactual and auditory), and the activity is related to the task being taught (reading). The second point is a less obvious one but is worth underlining. All the activities exercise different aspects of reading, but never in isolation. Each of the activities maintains a 'feel' of reading.

CHAPTER 5

Optimizing the use of sensory information

Michael Tobin

Introduction

One of the ways in which we can conceptualize the role of the teacher of children with multiple disabilities, and especially those with sensory impairments, is in terms of optimizing the children's physical environment and of enhancing their sensory functioning. The contents and the layout of the classroom and play area, and the activities the teacher wants to be undertaken by a child, are typically designed to strike a balance between motivating the child to explore and to undergo new experiences on the one hand, and avoiding a plethora of objects and activities that might overwhelm the child and make it impossible for him or her to differentiate among them. The optimal environment may be described as one where consistency and novelty are sufficiently well balanced for the sensorily impaired child to be able to operate within it and develop an internal, mental representation of it. This representation will allow the child to cope with changes or challenges in the real environment, and will stimulate him or her to use sight, touch, hearing, taste and smell to identify new objects or new examples of those with which s/he is already familiar.

For those severely visually impaired children who have some potentially useful sight – and they are almost certainly the majority – the realization of this potential depends upon four factors: the accurate diagnosis of the impairment; the prescribing and regular use of spectacles and other low-vision aids that will bring about the sharpest image on the retina; structured experiences and training in 'learning to look'; and a visual environment where colour, brightness, contrast, and image size are optimal for the child and his or her individual needs. The issue now to be addressed is whether microcomputer technology may have, as its advocates maintain, a part to play in optimizing this visual environment.

The argument put forward in support of the claim is based upon two characteristics of the technology, viz.: the computer's visual display unit (the VDU) and its 'menu' system. The VDU is a light-emitting rather than a light-reflecting device. It does not matter how close the user brings his or her eyes to the screen; s/he cannot (as with light-reflectors such as the page of a book or a projector screen or a chalk-board) inadvertently block the light source with his or her head, and so reduce the amount of light reaching the eyes. In addition, of course, the user can control the brightness and contrast levels to suit his or her own idiosyncratic preferences. The 'menu' that is part and parcel of well-designed computer software can be used by the visually impaired person to select colours (of both the image and its background), print sizes and shapes, and the speed and duration of images that best suit his or her visual abilities. The options available on the menu also provide the teacher with a means of exploring various combinations of brightness, size, colour, and other variables with a view to making decisions about effecting improvements in learning.

If the technologists' claims are valid in relation to optimizing visual environments, do they hold up, too, vis-à-vis hearing and touch? In the classroom, teachers know what an optimized tactile environment requires. It consists of objects whose size, shape, weight, hardness, and textures make it possible for them to be readily discriminated from one another and identified. Similarly, an optimized auditory environment presupposes adequate differentiation in terms of loudness, pitch, duration, and other characteristics of auditory stimuli. If the young child is to discriminate among, learn about, and use the objects and events of the physical world, then the important, the uniquely determining, features of these phenomena must be salient and brought specifically to his or her attention. This entails parents and teachers presenting them in such a way as to make them as easily apprehendable as possible by his or her senses, especially when one or more of these senses may be defective.

At present, it is not quite so easy to argue that technology performs an optimizing function in relation to the non-visual modalities, especially touch and hearing. It can nevertheless be claimed that tactile and auditory peripherals (for example, touch tablets and synthetic speech devices that are under the immediate control of the user) make it possible to modulate the speed, duration, and intensity of outputs to accord with his or her abilities and needs.

It is even harder at present to say whether using microcomputers brings about permanent improvements in sensory functioning in human beings. It is now well-established, at least at the infra-human level, that inadequate stimulation at critical, early stages of development can have deleterious consequences: Hubel and Wiesel (1963) demonstrated that newly-born kittens deprived of light for several weeks were unable to develop normal vision (but such deprivation did not have similar harmful effects on adult cats). It has also been shown that the human brain is affected by prolonged use of parts of the external sensori-motor system. For example, Pascual-Leone and Torres (1993) reported enlargement of the area of the cortex which 'maps' the right (reading) index finger of braillists (as compared with the area mapping the non-reading left index finger-tip and with both corresponding areas in non-braillists). These differences were not, however, associated with 'differences in the sensory, touch and two-point discrimination thresholds between the reading and the non-reading fingers' (p.49).

In the absence of clear-cut theoretical and empirical evidence to support the notion that microcomputers have some part to play in improving functioning, it may be safer, at present, to base the claim for improvement in performance upon rather general – non-physiological – arguments to do with the value of repeated practising of skills and of their refinement and strengthening. The computer can be programmed to provide opportunities for practice, and also to give immediate feedback to the learner about the correctness or otherwise of his or her responses; both these features are known to be conducive to successful learning. Carefully designed practice exercises can also direct the learner's attention to the significant features of the whole stimulus array, by giving them greater amplitude, permanently or sporadically, as against the non-meaningful stimuli.

In this chapter, evidence will be presented from classroom experience to support the claim that microcomputers can be used for engineering an enhanced sensory environment. The issue of long-term improved functioning will be addressed, even if not definitively substantiated, by experience based upon objective classroom observations. In emphasizing classroom-based evidence, the intention is to focus attention upon the contributions of the teacher and the learner rather than of the technologist. The teacher has to set the teaching and learning objectives, determine the extent to which a particular piece of software accords with those objectives, and then regulate the timing of its use. More importantly, s/he will want to capitalize upon what the child has learned and help him or her to apply it to other situations, as it will be this 'transfer' and extension of learning that will be the ultimate test of the technology's value. For the child, the excitement of using the technology will enhance what it objectively offers: control, options in accord with his or her sensory needs, and immediate feedback about the adequacy of responses. Unless these interactive opportunities are grasped, there can be no possibility of substantive, progressive learning being achieved.

Of course, such learning will depend too upon basic organizational matters to do with the kinds of devices being used and their placing in the classroom. As some of the following case studies will suggest, account may have to be taken of the height of the VDU if pupils with physical disabilities are to be able to scan the images on the screen without discomfort. It may be necessary for central or free-standing lighting to be switched off or dimmed so that it does not distract the child who is sensitive to light. Children with poor hand and finger control may need to control the computer by means of touch tablets with large panels responsive to gross hand movements. Where should the tablet be placed, in front or to one side of the computer? If in front, will this mean that the screen will be now too far away? If to one side, will this interfere with the co-ordination of hand and eye movements? Speech synthesizers may guide the learner in searching for information on the screen, and teachers may have to help the child with mild or moderate hearing loss to come to terms with the unusual quality of this synthetic speech. In other words, the teacher must have the time, and appropriate training, to become familiar with the control and management of the technology, so that s/he can adapt existing classroom teaching skills to the new situation.

Optimizing the environment

An example of how an appropriate visual environment can be productive in changing a child's behaviour is the case of Nicoll, a six-year old developmentally young child with profound hearing loss, very limited vision and low muscle tone. He was hyper-distractible, unable to ignore any passing stimulus and frequently distracted by his own arm and leg movements. His attention span was approximately 5-10 seconds. He gazed at any direct or reflected light, and would stare into a television screen, although he did not appear to focus on complex or fast-moving images.

Nicoll's teacher wanted to achieve two objectives with the computer: firstly, she wanted Nicoll to have the experience of attending for longer than ten seconds; and secondly, she wanted to see whether he could control the computer. (Although Nicoll had some understanding of cause-and-effect, his distractibility generally prevented him from controlling his environment.)

The computer was set up in a small bare room with no external light source. Nicoll's seating was adjusted to bring him in line with the screen whilst sitting fully supported, and initially he was given a grip to hold with each hand to help him stay still. His teacher selected programs showing clear, simple images with high contrast and lots of red and yellow (Nicoll's favourite colours). The images moved slowly around the screen.

At first Nicoll was so excited that it was impossible to tell whether he preferred any image to any other. Over time, however, it became clear that he did have favourites, and his attention to these images lasted considerably longer than usual – approximately 25-30 seconds. One grip was replaced with a switch, and Nicoll successfully took control of the images' movement. At this stage his teacher tried introducing some natural light to the room, but Nicoll's distress indicated that he preferred the conditions previously established. He extended his control, however, by turning and prodding the teacher whenever he wanted the program changed – showing an understanding that she had not predicted.

Similar benefits were obtained by Peter, a cognitively able eight year old who was profoundly deaf and had minimal vision. He was photophobic (bright light caused him discomfort and pain), and under normal conditions could perceive magnified symbols or pictures only with high figure-ground contrast (for example, black symbols on a white or yellow background). He had difficulty in shifting his visual attention from one item to another, and was slow to focus.

Peter enjoyed working at the computer, and he and his teacher worked cooperatively to optimize his learning environment. They very quickly established that the brightness control needed to be turned to 'low', and the contrast to maximum. Peter could use any number of switches, and could make some use of the computer keyboard, but either of these meant that he had to focus, press the switch or key, then shift attention to the screen and re-focus – by which time the relevant image had often come and gone. Using a touchscreen minimized these problems. His teacher identified touchscreen programs with menus allowing the screen colours to be changed, and Peter suggested different colour combinations to try. He was delighted to find that the backlighting of the screen enabled him to work with a far wider range of colour combinations – identifying, for example, a slowly moving pale green star on a yellow background.

Peter's teacher felt that one valuable outcome related to Peter's preparation for independence. He had worked with her, negotiating and discussing how best to use an aid to meet his specific needs – a skill essential for any able deaf-blind adult. The computer provided the motivational power and flexibility without which the negotiation could not have occurred.

Painter (1984) has described the use of a screen-based software package allowing letters, words, and digits to be varied in size, spacing, and colour (including the facility to change the background colour) with twenty learners with visual impairments and multiple disabilities. The purpose was to determine the 'smallest size shapes readable' and the most comfortable size of task for each of the subjects. In addition, all five text sizes (from 9 mm up to 54 mm) were presented to determine whether increasing the size of characters led eventually to a decrease in performance.

Painter reported that the results were 'very revealing', with most pupils able to 'read much smaller size characters' than the teachers had predicted, and that most learners 'were much more comfortable with the smaller size'. Nevertheless, 'the average size print with which the majority were most comfortable when reading was approximately 18 mm. What was of special interest here was that in a follow-up study, with the print now being on paper rather than on the VDU, the students 'were more comfortable with a slightly larger size'. This suggests that the computer-controlled format enhanced the visual decoding/recognition process to the extent that the readers could cope with reduced size and judged themselves to be more at ease, less severely stretched, in that environment. When reverting to 'hard copy' format (the printed page), they lacked the other attributes of the optimized, screen-based presentation, and therefore required an enlarged print to compensate for the absence of these attributes.

Another example of the possible beneficial effects of this kind of enhanced visual environment is given by Spencer and Ross (1989) who hypothesized that

> some children who are close to the threshold between sight and no sight [may be able to] 'see' images on a microcomputer screen while not being able to 'see' conventional media.
>
> (Spencer and Ross, 1989, p.69)

They cite the case of a fifteen year old boy at a school for blind children with additional disabilities:

> who was considered to have no sight and was being taught purely by tactile means. When, by chance, he was presented with a small yellow triangle (about 40 mm high) on a BBC microcomputer screen, he remarked, 'What's that yellow triangle?'.
>
> (Spencer and Ross, 1989, p.69)

Having acknowledged that the concepts of triangle and yellow must have been learned somehow (triangle possibly from directed tactual exploration and yellow from what they call 'incidental learning'), they go on to speculate whether, if the boy's ability to see images on a computer screen had been identified earlier, his visual skills could have been developed sooner and more effectively. Of major interest, though, is the possible implication that the concept of triangle may have been generalized across sensory modalities. If the boy's visual capabilities had been assessed earlier in a way relevant to classroom activities (as opposed to the somewhat artificial setting of the ophthalmic clinic with its requirements for standard distances and standard lighting levels), then higher levels of functioning might have been revealed, giving rise to higher expectations and demands. In the absence of this kind of comprehensive visual assessment, it is not possible to claim with any certainty that generalization and transfer had occurred; an alternative explanation is that he had always used his residual vision when learning by touch, and this practice had not been recognized by his parents and teachers. In other words, caution has to be exercised when inferring that an optimized visual environment has facilitated generalization and transfer from learning acquired through other sensory channels.

For many children with visual impairment, the optimizing of the visual environment is largely a built-in feature of the hardware, the CCTV and VDU devices which they use. For younger, or less able, children, it is not quite so much a case of their being taught to control the devices to meet their own idiosyncratic visual needs. It depends, rather, upon their teachers selecting for them the combination of learning activities and technological options that constitute the optimal environment. Alex, for example, was a three-year old girl with limited vision due to optic atrophy, and a history of frequent stays in hospital. She had to sit on her teacher's lap, with both of them, to begin with, using their fingers for touching and controlling the touch-sensitive screen so that coloured squares could be made to appear and disappear. Alex's very poor colour sense was such that she initially displayed no consistency at all in attaching colour names to the three-dimensional objects in the classroom ('yellow' shelves for housing all yellow objects, for example) but the screen-based two-dimensional images led to significant improvements, with teacher and child feeling and examining objects and then searching for their two-dimensional counterparts on the screen. Here, the learning was characterized by the teacher/child interactions, with the teacher capitalizing upon any objects at hand in the classroom, upon her and Alex's use of language to guide the searching, and upon the images stored in the computer.

Improving sensory functioning

If we take the more cautious approach of claiming that enhanced sensory functioning is in part the outcome of practice, feedback, and the learning and faster recognition of the significant elements of stimuli, then there is convincing case study evidence of the value of technology in mediating these processes. This approach relieves us of the necessity to demonstrate that visual acuity, tactual thresholds and auditory discrimination have been affected in any measurable way. The analogies that are appropriate here are those to do with perfecting the backhand stroke in tennis, or with learning to drive a car, and not with the improving of visual acuity with spectacles or the enhancing of hearing by means of hearing aids.

One measure of a child's progress is when s/he becomes bored with tasks that seemed initially too difficult. Four-year old Charles, with minimal expressive language skills and unwilling to move from one room to another without adult guidance, illustrates this phenomenon. His ocular albinism caused low vision and photophobia (discomfort in bright light), and made him uncomfortable when confronted with a brightly-lit VDU. Even when the brightness control knob was used to lower the intensity he still initially had problems with visual training/stimulation software of the least demanding nature (RCEVH Just Look and RCEVH Just Touch and Touch It). Increasing confidence, based presumably upon his growing ability to control these simple programs, led him eventually to by-pass the easier repetitive pointing options in their menus, and to take over from his teacher, with her directing and supporting language becoming less necessary.

This is a stage further on from that described by Bozic et al., (1993) where the teacher's use of language is believed to be one of the key elements in enabling the child to understand the nature of the task, and where the repetitiveness of the screen-based activities provides a predictable routine and structure. Charles's desire to move on to more perceptually and cognitively complex activities was seen as proof that some form of 'habituation' had occurred in relation to the simpler tasks. This in itself suggests that he had developed the visual fixation, identification, and left-to-right scanning required to achieve success at the lower levels sufficiently to use them for higher level operations involving hand-eye co-ordination, visual memory, and selective attention and comparison. These improvements were accompanied by demands, expressed verbally and by pulling the teacher's hand, to go to the 'puter' room each day.

We may be seeing something similar with the case of Gary, reported by Aitken and McDevitt (1995, Book 3, p.15). Gary had low vision and multiple disabilities, and his teacher's challenge was to help him switch attention among 'different visual stimuli and to associate his actions with effects'. Touch Games 1 with its graded programs enabled Gary to move on from merely touching the screen (whereupon an object appeared) to having 'to "take" with his finger a honey bee to a flower'. The fixating of attention is a prerequisite of more complex visual skills, which are called upon 'on the same disc (to) help to improve memory and visual discrimination'. Again, emphasis is placed upon the role of the teacher's and the child's language in supporting the development of visual and psychomotor skills. The brief case study of Gary concludes 'Now that he is predicting how to use the programs, he will move on to use Touch Fun Fair'. The case study brings out the interdependence of sensory modalities, and the extent to which looking is therefore capable of being enhanced in its effectiveness by information from touch and hearing.

Conclusion

As the RNIB survey (Walker et al., 1992) has shown, around 56 per cent of all visually impaired children have additional disabilities, with nearly half of that group having three or more additional impairments. The diversity of their needs makes it difficult to draw up a common curriculum, let alone a common methodology of teaching. What modern technology may be able to offer is a means of improving the overlap in the information coming in through the defective sensory channels. It can, too, make possible the modulation of the quality or intensity of the stimuli arriving via a particular channel, and this may enhance the learning environment for the child.

It can be argued that this is really no more than an extension of what teachers of children with visual impairments and multiple disabilities do as a matter of routine, and that technology is therefore just an additional means of attaining long-standing objectives. Where it may be said to differ is in its precision and its speed. Peter's needs for maximum contrast and lower levels of brightness could be met by the turning of two control knobs. Alex's problems with colour discrimination and colour naming were tackled by a combination of classroom and computer-based activities, with the latter being characterized by immediate feedback to her about the correctness of her responses, and with, of course, the facility for prolonged practice until she felt confident in her ability to cope with this sort of task.

From the teacher's vantage point, what is required is a mixture of so-called framework software (the actual pedagogical content of which can be put in quite easily by the teacher after minimal training) and predesigned, fully worked out teaching/learning programs that provide learner- and teacher-controlled options for altering the sensory environment visually, tactually, and auditorily. However, if these facilities are to be anything more than a way of making computer-based activities more accessible and exciting (and perhaps useful time-filling supplements while other classmates' individual needs are attended to), then the training needs of the teachers must be addressed in a systematic manner. In-service courses should be devised to allow teachers and software designers to interact and explore together the possibilities, and the limits, of the technology. Teachers who have used programs must be encouraged on these courses to share their experience of successes and failures with their colleagues, and provide examples of how they have integrated technology into the daily routine of a class of children with multiple disabilities, whose developmental growth does not follow a smooth predictable path of ever increasing competence.

Acknowledgements

I would like to thank Chris Painter of Condover Hall School for his assistance.

Part 2
Learning in technological environments

CHAPTER 6

Social interaction in multi-sensory environments

Sheila Glenn, Cliff Cunningham and Alison Shorrock

Introduction

Children with profound and multiple learning disabilities (PMLD) present a particular challenge to those who work with them. Profound motor, sensory and intellectual disabilities may result in an apparent lack of responsiveness towards both people and objects. This makes the design of therapeutic programmes difficult; furthermore, assessment of progress is often disappointing when conventional assessment devices are used.

We can, however, gain some information from studies of early development in children without disabilities. Advances in theoretical concepts and methodologies over the last forty years have shown that at least from birth onwards (and possibly earlier), infants show considerable competencies in perception, learning and memory, and perhaps particularly in the social domain. Studies of this kind have used quite specialized techniques to tap their understanding of the world; for example how infants perceive, remember and learn to control both their social and object environments. Such studies indicate methods and theories which might be used in studying children with PMLD who are also at very young developmental levels. These children are not the same as infants, of course. For one thing, they have lived for much longer, and had far more experiences. We would argue, however, that there is some benefit in applying the same methods and concepts when studying children with very severe disabilities.

There is a paucity of research on the development of children with PMLD. We need far more studies to determine underlying competencies in both social and object interaction. In addition, we need to see how these competencies are used in everyday life, as research in the classroom has shown an extreme lack of response to social initiations made by children with PMLD, together with low overall rates of social interaction

(Ware, 1994). If children perceive that they cannot control their environment, there is a risk of the development of 'learned helplessness' (Seligman, 1975): prolonged exposure to non-contingency may result in reduced motivation to act on the environment. This in turn may cause actions to be turned in on the self, resulting in an increase in self-stimulation.

We also know from work on early development that infants are born with abilities particularly geared toward encouraging and supporting social interactions. A major question for us, then, has been how to let a child (with PMLD) demonstrate competencies in a social environment which is relatively insensitive to his or her damaged, distorted or minimal social signals. This problem is compounded by the fact that at very young developmental levels nondisabled children are usually in a very familiar environment, with only a few highly constant caregivers who know them and their past history very well. Such familiarity in social routines is a major factor in the social/emotional motivational development of children in the first year of life.

This is probably even more important for children with PMLD with their limited information processing capacities; if they take longer to learn, they will be more dependent on consistent signals from others, and furthermore will also be dependent on others' ability to 'read' their signals and respond appropriately and consistently.

In this context, the spread of multi-sensory environment centres in the UK is seen as a potentially important development (Hutchinson and Kewin, 1994). The initial emphasis of such centres was on the provision of leisure and pleasure in a secure, socially interactive situation. However, they also provide a wide range of sensory stimulation and some opportunity for children to exert control over their environment through specialized equipment. Thus there is an important combination of social and object interaction, and opportunities to express choice. This redirects the emphasis of activities from structured teacher-led programmes towards flexible child-led activity, supported by a more able other (adult or peer). This chapter describes ongoing research in such a centre.

The chapter is divided into three sections:

- A discussion of what our aims for children with PMLD might be.
- A description of the abilities that might be expected very early in development, and whether these have also been demonstrated in children with PMLD.
- A description of current research in a multi-sensory environment.

Educational aims for children with PMLD

Ware (1994) argues that within the National Curriculum new aims need to be developed, as otherwise for year after year children are simply assessed as working towards the lowest level. This is extremely disheartening for both parents and teachers.

She believes that when we work with children with PMLD we should be enabling them to participate as far as possible in what happens to them. She argues that the problem of access to the National Curriculum is qualitatively different from that of other children with less severe learning difficulties. One major problem identified by teachers of this group is that access to key experiences considered essential for all human beings is extremely difficult. One of these key issues is relationships with others. It is thus disturbing that Evans and Ware (1987), in a study of children in Special Care Units in the South East of England, found that teachers reported that 80.9 per cent of the children had no communication skills. Whether they had or not, what is important is that teachers believed they did not, and it is likely that this belief influenced teachers' interactions with these children (Goldbart, 1994). Newson (1978) states, '[I]t is only because he [the child] is treated as a communicator that he learns the essential human art of communication' (p.42). Thus teachers' beliefs that children with PMLD cannot communicate may result in fewer attempts to interact.

Some support for this view was found by Ware (1994); in four classes for children with PMLD studied over a period of time, the majority of interactions were very brief, lasting less than one minute. Interaction occurred on average only once every twelve to thirteen minutes. When interacting the adults rarely behaved as though they expected a response, and they rarely responded to a pupil's initiation. Ware showed that interactions could be influenced by staff training, and that there was some indication of enhanced pupil progress as a result. In addition, training was more successful if individual child-staff pairs were targeted initially.

Our own interest lies in looking at the nature of interactions in a leisure-oriented multi-sensory setting, to see if more behaviour results when supported by other involvement.

Early abilities

There are two main perspectives:

- Those theories which look primarily at infants' understanding of the nonsocial environment.
- Those theories which emphasize the social context of development.

Piaget's theory (1953b) is an example of the former perspective. In this theory the first stage of development is from primary circular reactions, where a child is primarily concerned with his or her own body, to secondary circular reactions, where the child begins to act on the environment to produce reactions. This happens at around 3 to 4 months of age in normal development, and is a sign that the child is beginning to realize that the self is separate from the environment.

This has also been described as the beginning of contingency awareness (Watson, 1972), i.e. the child acts, and has sufficient memory and processing ability to register that his or her actions result in an effect. However, Watson has also argued that this stage occurs earlier for social interaction than object interaction – for example, infants look at people, who often start talking and smiling in response; infants make a noise and people respond; infants smile and usually get major responses; infants make a face or a noise and mothers often imitate them. The infant soon learns that his or her behaviour can 'control' that of others. Theorists such as Ainsworth (1982) argue that a feeling of efficacy first develops through this awareness of social control.

Thus there has been a move in recent years to incorporate into educational programmes theories which emphasize the social context of development: for example, the work of Vygotsky (1978). This theory holds that infants do not develop in isolation, but through interaction with more competent others (parents, teachers, more able peers). The theory argues that learning is first achieved via social mediation, with the child subsequently internalising what has been learned in a social context. Kaye (1982) notes that 'Adults provide an environment within which the infant's sensorimotor skills are adequate to certain tasks only because the adult breaks those tasks down and serves as the "memory" component of the infant's skill' (p.8). By reacting to the infant's behaviours as though they were meaningful and had intention, the parent lays the framework for the baby to learn about social systems. Without such expectations and interpretations the infant has no direction.

Studies of development

In a comprehensive review Bremner (1988) describes a large number of studies showing that from the first days of life infants can discriminate between stimuli and recognize and prefer their mother's voice and smell. From a few months they discriminate colours, shapes, faces, depth and many important speech sounds.

The methods developed to study young infants, who lack control over most movements and have very limited means of communication, can also be used to study children with PMLD. Unfortunately there is very little research in this area, but what there is indicates that these children do have similar abilities (see review by Shepherd and Fagan, 1981). Using such methods, e.g. the PLAYTEST, Glenn and Cunningham (1984a) showed that children with PMLD aged from 3 to 11 years, but functioning in the 3 to 12 months period developmentally, responded differentially to speech stimuli in the same way as 3 to 12 month old normally developing infants. This work supports the notion that children with PMLD, who are very young developmentally, are also more competent perceptually than is often assumed. It further indicates that these children are not mere passive recipients of stimulation, but active learners able to respond selectively to appropriately selected activities (Glenn and Cunningham, 1984b). Such findings support the argument that our knowledge of typical early behaviour can inform the content of the curriculum for children with PMLD.

How the information is presented is equally important. DeCasper and Carstens (1981), for example, demonstrated that infants in the first weeks of life are responsive to contingencies. They point out that:

> It is important to note that attention, positive affect, and lack of fear arise because of the contingent nature of stimulation; that inattention, neutral affect, and depression arise from non-contingent stimulation; and that fear and negative affect arise because the nature of the contingency is, momentarily, uncertain or ambiguous. (p.20)

Sensory stimulation which is unresponsive to the child's behaviour may therefore be less than helpful. Brinker and Lewis (1982) concluded from a study of contingency in young children with severe learning disability that 'handicapped infants may begin to lose interest in a world which they do not expect to control' (p.164).

This view derives from the perspective which stresses the importance of children *acting* on their environments, not just perceiving them (Piaget 1953b). Essentially the argument is that if children have few opportunities to act to control the environment (because of disability or deprivation), then they will have difficulty in developing contingency awareness, and will be less motivated to act in future (Glenn and O'Brien 1994).

O'Brien et al. (1994) studied seven infants and children with severe, profound and multiple learning disabilities (chronological age 3 months to 4 years, mean mental age 4.5 months). A microcomputer was used to mediate between the child's response – a leg or arm movement to break a light sensitive beam – and environmental effects. In this way, children were presented with a contingency situation where they controlled the onset of a visually and auditorily attractive toy. In this situation their responding increased, and some positive emotional effects were seen. When the situation was changed so that they could no longer control the stimulation, negative effects were seen on a range of emotional, motivational and self-stimulation measures. It was concluded from these results that from a developmental age level of at least 2 months children, regardless of disabilities, are equipped to detect cause-and-effect relationships and to build up a picture of their world based on expectancies about such relationships. Having established such expectations, they become upset and fearful if these are not met with some regularity – as appears to be common in many everyday settings (Evans and Ware, 1987).

O'Brien et al's study again demonstrated learning competencies in children with PMLD, but in an experimental, specialized situation. We need more information about how such abilities function in more complex and naturalistic settings. The studies outlined above mainly concern object interactions and we also need more information about the opportunity early social interactions afford to learn about control. Although many teachers of children with PMLD do provide sensory stimulation in a way which is sensitive to children's responses (see Glenn, 1987, for a collation of practitioners' suggestions), we have little information about the nature of social interactions between these children and others.

We have argued that children with PMLD are similar to all infants in the early stages of development. They need social interactions which are tailored to their special needs, provide for contingent responsiveness to their output behaviours and allow them to feel that they control and understand their world. This places a special onus on their family and carers. How can they maintain and concentrate on such interactions in a busy ongoing situation? How can they engage together with the child on a task which is selected by, and controlled by, the child in the everyday setting?

Snoezelen or multi-sensory environments aim at providing a special situation appropriate to the developmental level of the person with PMLD, yet also amenable to others (Hulsegge and Verheul, 1987; Kewin, 1994). In theory such environments allow child and others to relax and engage with material, and interact in such a way that the quality of their interactions is improved. Each one can learn more about the other.

Work in multi-sensory environments

Multi-sensory rooms were first developed in the Netherlands in the 1970s; these were labelled 'Snoezelen': places where 'pleasurable experiences are generated in an atmosphere of trust and relaxation' (Kewin, 1994, p.8). The originators of the rooms emphasized the need to help clients gain maximum enjoyment and stimulation in a way chosen by them (Cunningham et al., 1991, Haggar and Hutchinson, 1991). There is some resistance to research and formal evaluations of these environments on the grounds that this would force clients into more structured, outcome-oriented work. In other words, the emphasis would be on work (by definition set from outside the individual), in contrast to play and freely chosen leisure (Hulsegge and Verheul, 1987). Furthermore, whilst no one disputes the importance of play and self-selected activities for young, normally developing children, all too often activities for those with disabilities have to be justified on therapeutic or educational grounds. The emphasis is frequently on teacher-selected, goal-oriented activities which are often then teacher-led, and this in turn is likely to reduce child control and spontaneity (Cunningham and Glenn, 1985).

However, research does not inevitably constrain or distort the evaluation of naturalistic or self-directed and spontaneous activity and should in fact contribute to the refinement and development of provision. In the current climate of accountability – and given the expense of multi-sensory environments – evaluation must be seen as an integral part of any organization which seeks to maintain itself and be adaptive.

At present there are few evaluation studies about these environments in the literature. Those that are available tend to be descriptive and to focus on adults (Hulsegge and Verheul, 1987; Hutchinson and Kewin, 1994). In an overview of the reports Cunningham et al., (1991) noted that several outcomes were claimed: people with PMLD enjoyed the environment and returned readily, exercised choice, became more relaxed and showed a reduction in stereotypic behaviour; parents and staff enjoyed being in the environment and found it relaxing; staff and carers reported that they gained new insights into the people with PMLD, and interactions and relationships changed in quality and became more positive. A recent study by Hutchinson and Haggar (1994) supports these claims.

We wanted to see if similar positive benefits could be demonstrated with children with PMLD and their parents attending a multi-sensory environment. Our research is described below.

Method

The Children

The children all had profound and multiple learning disabilities. There were three girls and two boys. Approximate developmental level was assessed on the Uzgiris and Hunt Scales (1975), Scale II: The development of means for obtaining desired environmental events. This was particularly problematic in the case of Jane, who had very severe cerebral palsy and little motor control; however she appeared to understand a great deal of what was said to her, and the assessment was primarily a reflection of her motor ability.

Child	Sex	Chronological Age	Estimated Developmental Age	Diagnosis
Jane	F	14 years	5 months	Cerebral Palsy due to prematurity. Unknown level of visual impairment
Susie	F	8.7 years	2 months	Anoxia at birth. Unknown level of visual impairment
Mary	F	4.5 years	4-5 months	Walker-Warburg Syndrome.
Daniel	M	11.2 years	9 months	Ringing of the 22nd chromosome
Edward	M	10.3 years	4-5 months	Smith Lernli Opitz Syndrome

Table 6.1: Details of children

From Table 6.1 it can be seen that in terms of their ability to act on the world the children were approximately in the 2 to 9 months developmental range. Daniel was the most advanced in terms of motor skills – he could move about unaided, whereas the other four children could not. Jane was the most advanced in terms of mental capacity, but unable to move unaided. Ability to act on the environment is what the assessments reflect.

All the parents had volunteered to bring the children to the SPACE

Centre for one hour a week over an eight week period. Two sessions were used to establish reliabilities. Not all attended all sessions due mostly to a high level of illness. Numbers of sessions reported for Jane, Susie, Mary, Daniel and Edward respectively are: 5, 3, 3, 6, 3.

The SPACE Centre

This consists of a soft-padded environment on two levels connected by a ramp and stairs. It has variable lighting and sound; there is also a ball pool, bubble tubes, a vibrating mat, a water bed, a plasma ball, a textured wall, fibre-optic lights, soft play equipment, a dark room with variable light stars, a soft cushion hammock which can be rotated and rocked, and soft toys designed to fluoresce in ultraviolet light.

Procedure

The first week was used as an introductory session. Parents were asked to look round the Centre and choose four activities which they thought would be particularly appropriate for their child. Daniel was allowed to move about freely and choose his own activities, but this was not possible for the other children who had to be moved manually.

At the first session each child was videotaped, and the four observers watched the tapes jointly in order to practise observations. As three of the observers were inexperienced it was decided to use time sampling of relatively simple behaviours. Observers each wore a personal stereo which indicated 15 second intervals at which behaviour had to be noted. Table 6.2 lists the behaviours that were recorded if they occurred.

Design

Four activities were chosen for the four non-mobile children, and the children were placed at these in a different order over each session.

Children stayed at each activity for ten minutes. Five minutes was spent with their parent (or in one case a brother) interacting with the child, and helping them with the activity, and five minutes was spent with the child alone at the activity. The order of the activities was counterbalanced over sessions. At the end of the forty minutes children were placed at the activity their parents chose, although, by this stage, most children were quite tired and appeared happy simply to relax. This design was believed to be sensitive to the interests of individual children, while providing enough structure to investigate the questions we were interested in.

Each child was always observed by the same observer.

Behaviour category	Includes:
Object interaction – all behaviours directed towards objects.	• Look at object. • Touch object. • Move as part of activity.
Positive emotional behaviour	• Smiling. • Happy noises.
Negative emotional behaviour	• Crying. • Moaning/unhappy noises.
Social interaction – all behaviour directed towards people.	• Look at person or other child. • Listen to another – usually indicated by stilling and orienting. • Touch another.
Respond	• Respond to another's initiation.
Initiate	• Initiate interaction (or try to do so).
Self stimulatory behaviour	• Any behaviour directed to own body stimulation.

Table 6.2: Observed behaviours

At the end of the eight week period parents and observers were asked to comment on their experiences.

Results

Behavioural measures

Figure 6.1 shows the average frequency of recorded behaviours (see Table 6.2) over sessions, for the two situations of interaction with others and alone.

Apart from Daniel, who is able to move unaided, and hence less dependent on social interaction, there are some clear differences between the situations with social interaction and those without. Jane, Susie, Mary

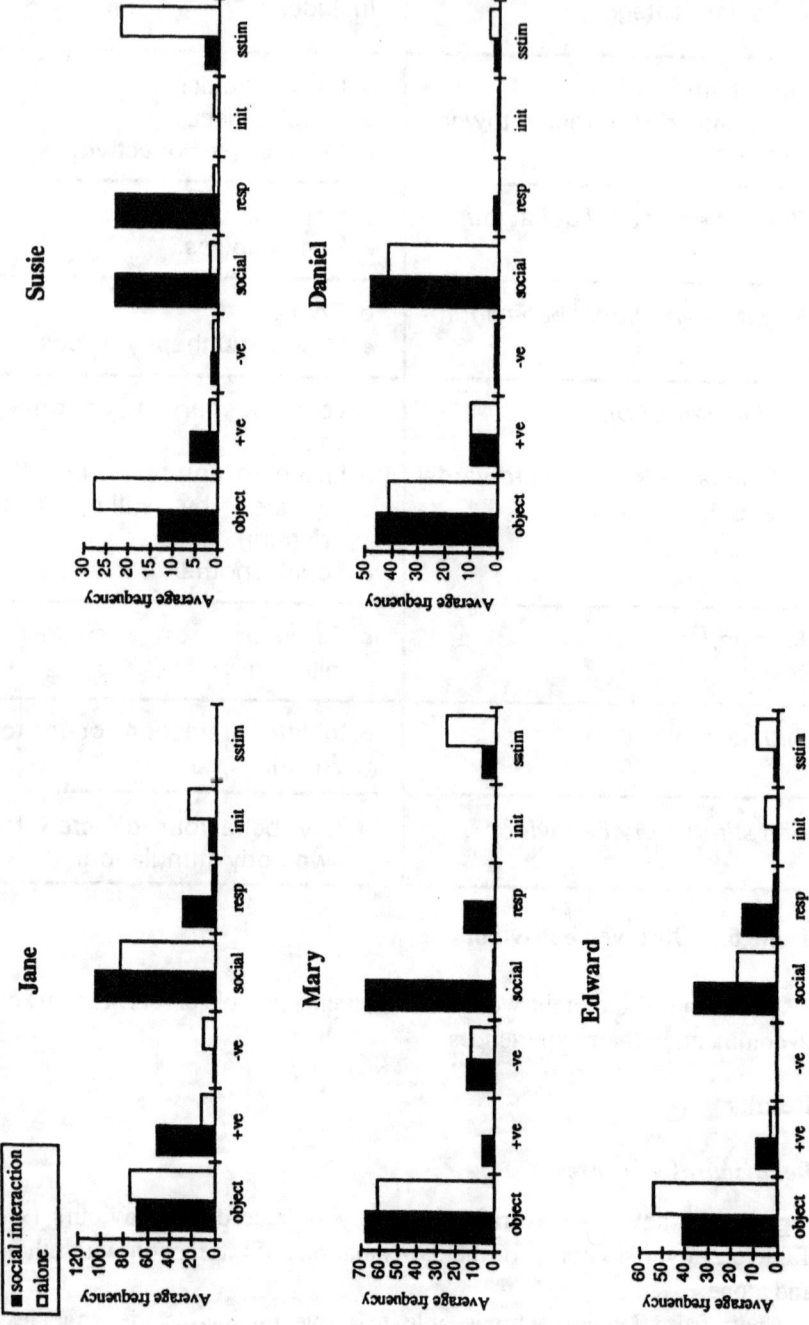

Figure 6.1: Average frequency of recorded behaviours in social interaction and alone situations

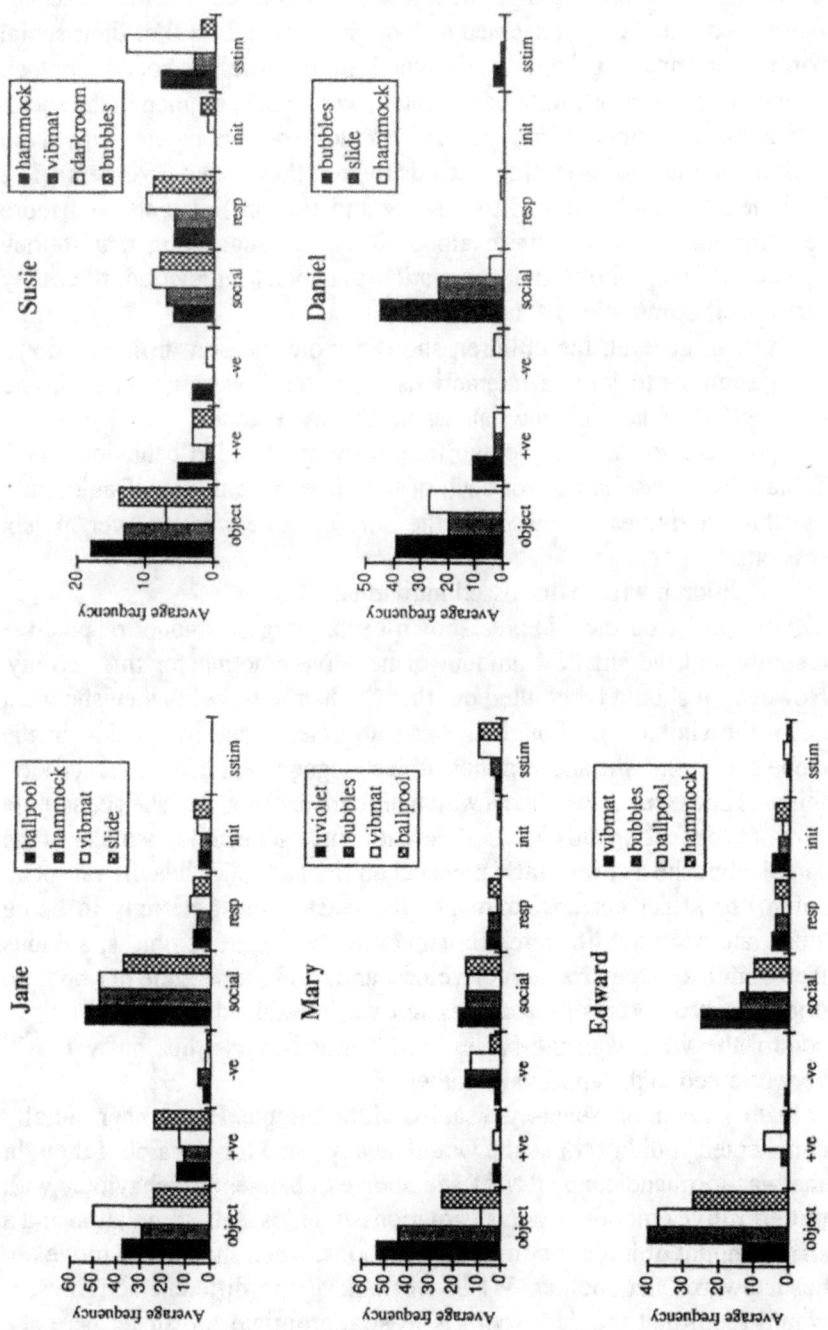

Figure 6.2: Average frequency of recorded behaviours for each activity

and Edward show more positive emotion in interaction. Jane, Susie and Edward show more attempts at initiations when they were in the no-interaction situations. It seemed as though the withdrawal of their social partner prompted behaviour designed to re-establish social contact. Social behaviours, as might be expected, were more common in the social interaction situations. In alone situations most social behaviours involved looking at others or orienting towards them if they spoke (to others). The three least able children (Susie, Mary and Edward) also showed more self-stimulatory behaviour in alone situations, suggesting that if they cannot achieve control and stimulation via social interaction, then they turn to self-stimulation of their own bodies.

Thus, in general, the children showed more pleasure in interactions, more attempts to initiate interactions when these were terminated, and more self-stimulatory behaviour when they were alone.

Figure 6.2 shows the average frequency of recorded behaviours (see Table 6.2) over sessions, for each of the different activities. Daniel only has three activities, as these are the only ones he went to over his six sessions.

The children will be discussed individually.

Jane preferred the slide, as shown by the largest amount of positive emotion and the smallest amount of negative emotion for this activity. However, it should be pointed out that she had to be held when she went down the slide, even though she had no other social interaction in the alone condition. She showed most object engagement in the mat activity; this was because the mat had a wall hanging next to it, and she spent quite a lot of time feeling the objects. Jane is the most able child mentally in the sample, but she has very little physical ability and relies heavily on social control to affect her environment. She reacted most strongly to being alone and tried hard to re-establish contact by negative noises, anxious faces, smiles in the direction of voices, and trying to wriggle her body to orient towards others. At one session we introduced a touch switch to control the vibrating mat; she quickly learned to use this, but was still very oriented to the approval of others.

Susie is the most severely disabled of the sample. Her mother initially commented 'I didn't think she would be any good for research; I thought she was too handicapped'. Yet she showed changes in behaviour, with most positive emotion in social situations and most self-stimulation and a small amount of initiation in alone situations, when she tried to move her head towards her mother. When we look at the different activities, it would seem that the dark room is least appropriate for Susie; here she shows least activity and most self-stimulation. In contrast, at the bubble tubes and on the vibrating mat she showed least self stimulation, and quite a lot of attention, even in the alone condition. She cannot move her hands to touch, but did show a lot of mouthing. Although we called this self-stimulatory and it appeared most in the alone condition, it is possible that this is one of the few responses which may be under voluntary control, and therefore of use for contingency intervention.

Mary also only showed positive emotions in social situations, and far more self-stimulation in alone situations. She did not, however, try to initiate social contact when on her own. Work with objects fluorescing in ultraviolet light seemed to be her preferred activity. Here she showed most object involvement, least negative emotion, and least self-stimulatory activity. The bubble tubes were her second favourite, whereas she did not like the vibrating mat.

Daniel was relatively independent of the need for social support. His graph in Figure 6.1 shows little difference between social and nonsocial situations. He could move around, choose his own activities and look at others if he wished. This was in contrast to the other children, who were able to do very little without help. He had a very clear preference for the bubble tubes, showing most activity, most pleasure and most social behaviours in this situation. Quite often he would go to another child or adult who was at the bubble tubes, and look at them or touch them. He sat quite a lot and looked at others – this became more pronounced over sessions, and was seen as an advance by his mother who said that he never stayed still at home.

Edward also showed most pleasure in social situations, and least self-stimulation. He was very oriented towards his mother, touching and hugging her. He showed most activity at the bubble tubes and ballpool – reaching out to touch and bang, and most positive emotion was also seen in the ballpool. He did show some social responses in the alone situation, looking at others and touching his mother.

Mothers' views

At the last session mothers were asked about their feelings, and their impressions of the SPACE centre, and also for any suggestions that might improve the activities for them and their family.

Jane's mother

'We all enjoyed it. Jane did better when she had structure and help. She definitely improved – she was happier about being in the ball pool – and is now used to the quiet [alone] periods. We were pleased that she could do so much on her own'.

The value of SPACE for Jane and her family was captured by her nine year old brother who did a drawing of her in the centre. The caption read 'I like SPACE because I can have fun with Jane. I think she likes it because it gives her the freedom to play.'

Susie's mother

'She enjoyed it and so did I. I tell [Susie's sister] that this is the only place Susie can come and enjoy herself. She has Guides, horse-riding and so on, but Susie can't do anything like that. She liked the mat and the bubble tubes best'.

Mary's mother

Mary's mother was not present on the last occasion (her father was instead), so we could not ask her opinion. However she had said previously that she wanted Mary to 'improve' over the sessions; in other words, she was more oriented to a teaching role.

Daniel's mother

'Daniel really changed over the weeks we came. He moves round all the time at home, but here after a few weeks he became much quieter and sat still and looked at things. He seemed really relaxed. We both enjoyed it a lot... We'll miss coming'.

Edward's mother

'It is interesting to watch his reaction. He knows where he is. It has been very useful and enjoyable. He has been a bit clingy – I think because he's not used to me being here. He has relaxed more and more – I was surprised how much he liked the ball pool by the end. I was a bit disappointed he wasn't more outgoing... It is good to meet the other parents. It's nice to be somewhere where your child isn't different'.

All the above comments support our observations that all the families enjoyed attending the centre. They also imply that parents gained new insights or perspectives about their children. Of particular interest is the number of parents who commented on the preferences their children showed for different activities, and how these confirm the observational data.

Possible changes

No parent suggested changes. Interestingly, all commented that they liked the structure of having four activities and limited time in each, but felt they would not want the activities themselves structured. All stated they would miss attending when the project ended. Many commented that their child enjoyed coming, and smiled when they arrived at the centre.

The observers reported that all the parents had great insight into their children and could certainly 'read' the child's behaviour far better than the observers in the first sessions – a skill which developed over time. In addition, the families treated their children as if their reactions were meaningful – for example, 'He's trying to tell me he doesn't like it', 'He wants me to pick him up', 'She's trying to get me to do it for her', 'He's telling me he's tired'.

Discussion

The most striking findings from these children with multiple disabilities were:

- All involved certainly appeared to enjoy their time in the multi-sensory environment.
- All the children showed a clear preference for specific activities, i.e. demonstrated an ability to choose.
- No one activity was preferred most by most children, which highlights the children's individuality and reinforces the notion that they selected their preferences.
- Those children who were most disabled were most dependent on affecting their environment by social means, illustrated by their attempts to re-establish social contact in the alone condition.
- Mothers' comments indicate that many formed new conceptions about their child – often seeing new abilities.

Thus, within the limitations of the study, these results add support to the previous descriptions of the benefits of such environments. It extends these to children and demonstrates the potential usefulness of observational methods for evaluation in these settings.

Perhaps the strongest impression left on us was the parents' affirmation that all their children were aware and responsive, and the way in which the multi-sensory environment enabled this to be seen. The children all showed responsivity when interacting with people who knew them and their social signals intimately, and who could themselves give appropriate and familiar social signals which were contingent on their child's behaviour.

Furthermore, by the second session all the observers said that they had become much more sensitive to the children's behaviours, as a result of seeing them interact with their parents.

Of course such impressions could be gained in the home or school setting. However, they are much easier to achieve in a purpose-built environment which all enjoy and hence which is more likely to facilitate such engagements. The parents were very relaxed and appreciative of a leisure facility suitable not only for the child with PMLD, but to which they could also bring other family members (brothers, sisters, fathers and grandmothers were involved over the weeks), and where they could engage in a relaxed way with their children and meet with other families.

What is now needed is more research on the effects on people less familiar with the children, to discover whether this relaxing, pleasure-oriented environment can encourage the development of social relationships and sensitivity, and hence provide the individual responsivity and increase in range of activities needed by children with PMLD.

Acknowledgements

Thanks are due to the parents and children for their willing participation, and to Dr Debbie Hews, Jane Glenn and John Kelly for giving their time to act as observers.

CHAPTER 7

Developing competencies in multi-sensory rooms

Richard Hirstwood and Clive Smith

Introduction

It is clear that multi-sensory rooms and their attendant technology are perceived to be major resources by many professionals working with people with learning disabilities. The multi-sensory room is perceived as a unique and invaluable asset in assisting those working with this group to achieve a wide variety of targets. The ideas and techniques discussed in this chapter are not exclusive to teachers in schools; parents, carers, nurses and others may find them equally appropriate. It is our contention that one of the greatest benefits of multi-sensory rooms is that they provide an environment in which everyone is learning, making everyone partners in the learning process.

Multi-sensory philosophies

A number of questions need to be addressed. What targets are appropriate for work in multi-sensory rooms? What is the role of multi-sensory technology in the teaching of children with multiple disabilities? How do these applications fit alongside the curricular requirements of schools?

There has been to date a philosophical rivalry within multi-sensory approaches that has polarized much of the work. The multi-sensory movement regularly cites the Hartenburg Institute as its birth place. The concept of Snoezelen (Hulsegge and Verheul, 1987) was developed and refined there, and underlies much of what could be termed the passive approach. However, during the same period, the growth of microtechnology was prompting an increase in switching as a discrete skill. From a variety of sources switches that could control mains-operated devices such as lights and tape recorders were developed. This route has been refined and developed into what is often termed the interactive approach. In our experience these approaches are compatible, and children will not only benefit from aspects of each, but should be given the opportunity to work in both modes if they are to gain fully from the advantages of multi-sensory technology. Multi-sensory rooms are places where teachers can control the child's environment closely; places where they can create the specific setting that they want for each individual.

Room design

It is clear that multi-sensory rooms, whilst varying greatly, do tend to have common elements. The equipment is housed in a room or area that can be blacked out, and generally includes items such as an effect projector, bubble tube, fibre-optic harness, mirror ball with coloured lights and a sound source such as a tape deck, music system or CD player. Whilst this technology is widely used, it must be recognized that there is a great deal of cheaper and simpler equipment that with skilful use can achieve the same ends.

Why use a multi-sensory technology?

Over the past decade, many schools for pupils with severe learning difficulties have seen an increase in the number of pupils with profound and multiple disabilities. Teachers have endeavoured to find materials, equipment and stimuli that these pupils will respond to, and that will motivate them to attempt to interact with the many different facets of their environment. Multi-sensory equipment provides powerful visual, aural and tactile stimuli, and gives the teacher control over the way in which the child's senses are affected. With the room blacked out, the teacher controls the location, type and quality of the light a child may see. The teacher can exercise similar control over sound, and tactile, olfactory and taste stimuli. External distractions are eliminated.

Effects of sensory stimuli

The other attractions of the room are far harder to explain in objective terms because they involve the way in which sensory stimuli affect our subconscious. Why, for example, are fish tanks placed in many dental reception areas? The light, the steady bubbles, the slowly moving, colourful fish, all combine to create a relaxing air. In contrast, the very powerful lighting effects that accompany any rock concert and even classical concerts are designed to stimulate and excite the audience. These effects typify the two extremes of the power of light in multi-sensory equipment. At one end of this spectrum effects are used which exaggerate and enhance our sensations, heightening our perceptions of a particular event, and at the other they subtly alter our perceptions, calming and moderating the fluctuations of our senses. It is the power of light and sound to affect the mind beyond its conscious level that forms the basis of much of the work within the sensory room. Similarly, sensory experiences of touch, smell and taste can provide sensations that are either relaxing or stimulating.

Implications of room design

The design of the multi-sensory room will affect a child's interpretation of the activities offered within it. Many rooms have white soft play covering on the floors, around the walls and even on the back of the door, with nothing to distinguish walls from floors, corners from walls. Contrasting colours of soft play may be introduced to provide points of reference, or cushions or drapes may distinguish corners and intersections between walls and floors. Individuals with visual impairments may gain their points of reference from available light, and will benefit greatly from having different coloured light sources in front and to the sides. They can then define their own spatial position in terms of the position of coloured lighting; the blue light in front and green and red light to opposite sides. Now think of the lighting effects used in multi-sensory rooms which cycle through a colour sequence, and of the confusion caused when green is now in front and blue to the side and so on. Through the room design, we may be communicating confusion. There is a tendency to assume that children using multi-sensory rooms perceive and interpret them in the same way that we do, forgetting that our cognitive skills allow us to interpret what is happening far more easily.

The way that we position children will also affect their responses. A child may not respond to an effect or to the teacher simply because all his or her concentration is being used on keeping upright, or waiting for the next sudden movement caused by someone walking past. This will happen frequently if other people are moving around on a fully covered soft play floor, and will require the child to make constant bodily adjustments. The comfort of water beds, similarly, may be outweighed by a feeling of not being in control. Lack of personal control is almost guaranteed to cause tension, and if you are worrying about what will happen to you next, you are unlikely to listen or take in anything that is communicated to you. Water beds, hammocks and leaf chairs, whatever their positive qualities, must come high on any list of furniture endangering feelings of being in control.

Many of these aspects should be considered at the planning stage, but in the search for the ideal, compromises in room design must obviously be made. It is up to staff to consider these factors within each individual's personal programme for the multi-sensory room, and to arrive at the best solution for each individual's needs.

What can we do with multi-sensory rooms?

Multi-sensory rooms may be used for work towards a range of educational targets. We will consider three examples: relaxation skills, cause-and-effect work and communication.

Relaxation skills

The ability to relax is a crucial skill for everyone. For individuals who are able to exercise free choice relaxation is difficult enough, but for those whose multiple disabilities restrict free choice the physical and mental manifestations of stress may eventually surface. It is possible that as teachers we are familiar with the evidence of stress, but that we provide alternative labels such as self injury, aggressive behaviour, or stereotypical mannerisms. As a life skill, relaxation is as important as educational targets couched in curricular terms.

Multi-sensory rooms incorporate a wide range of effects generally considered to be restful. Subjective and anecdotal evidence suggests that they may help children to become considerably calmer, less agitated, less tense and more peaceful.

Case study: Barry

Barry is fifteen and large for his age. No toys, equipment or other environmental artefacts have ever kept his interest on other than a perfunctory level, and attempts to direct his activities both educationally and simply to keep him safe have often led to violent outbursts resulting in various forms of control.

When the school installed a multi-sensory room, Barry's class (a group needing special care) was one of the first groups targeted, and the pupils were taken in as a group. Barry was quickly excluded from this session as he spent his time in the sensory room stumbling about, especially on the soft play floor, falling onto children and equipment. The risk of injury to himself and other children was too great, given the supervision that could be provided for the full class.

After a while the group's session was reduced as it became clear that the class did not benefit from a complete hour, and the remainder of the session was used to give Barry time alone in the room with his teacher.

The first thing the teacher did was to lift the soft play up from the floor and stand it against the wall. This meant that Barry's mobility difficulties were not as great, and it had a further advantage. When the room was dark he had difficulty assessing the limits of the room, and frequently walked into the wall. The soft play positioned against the wall now cushioned the impact of this. In his first sessions all the equipment, bubble tube, fibre-optics, projector and music were put on at the same time. It became obvious that Barry was attracted to the light, as he moved continually around the room from one effect to another but paused for some moments at each lighting effect. The teacher then decided to put just one effect on at a time and see how Barry responded. His movement continued, albeit at a much reduced level, but he spent an increasing amount of time with each effect. A further modification was made to the room by turning around the soft play mats leaning against the wall. The white mats had a black rubberized base, and this reduced the amount of reflected light elsewhere in the room and emphasized the effect of the light source being used. Barry seemed to prefer the bubble tube, as this was the first effect at which he actually sat down, and the one where he spent increasingly longer periods of time. After several sessions Barry started to sit down directly in front of the bubble tube as soon as it was switched on. His teacher sat with him, talking gently, but making no demands. However, if Barry looked at or turned to another effect, she switched off the one he had been looking at and immediately went and switched on the one that he had turned to. The result of this experimentation was that Barry was much calmer in these sessions and stopped his rather frantic movement.

It became clear to Barry's teacher that, for whatever reason, the room provided an environment which Barry found calming, comforting and safe, and one in which he showed the first evidence of interest in his environment. It was also one in which long-established barriers could be broken down. Because of Barry's challenging behaviour, his teacher was regularly faced with negative situations in which she felt that no progress was being made. Now, however, as a result of his calmer behaviour in the room, his teacher began to view him in a positive light, and was more than happy to work with him in a one to one situation. A far greater degree of positive interaction occurred within the multi-sensory room than had previously happened in any other setting.

Whilst it was very difficult at the outset for his teacher to put to one side the notion that she should be proactive, always initiating developments, she realized that in this atmosphere Barry himself had begun to show positive initiations. He started to look for the other pieces of equipment in the darkness of the room, clearly indicating that he was remembering where they were, instead of just happening upon objects as he had always done in the classroom. When he began to look for other pieces of equipment, the teacher responded by switching off the current effect and putting on the next. Soon Barry was looking with intent at whatever piece of equipment he wanted switched on. For the first time in his eleven years within the school, staff perceived Barry as a communicator.

Discussion

The changes in Barry's behaviour seem due to both the power of the equipment to present a relaxing environment, and the way in which staff interacted with him whilst in the multi-sensory room. We have found similar results in other establishments working with children and adults with challenging behaviour (Smith, 1993) and there has also been significant success in helping children and adults with autism who displayed the same forms of behaviour. The process is not simply one of 'laissez faire' and there are obvious dangers in using the room as a 'super time out room'. It may seem to be stating the obvious that the first step is to provide an environment that is relaxing, but this will not be the same for every individual. Staff must assess which aspects of the room an individual likes. Do they like being in a dark room? Some children will find this threatening. Do they like blue lights, or do they prefer red? What sort of music do they prefer? There must be an assessment of the child's preferences for positioning, lighting, music and the time for using the room. We do not relax at 10.30 on Tuesday morning because that is our relaxing time!

The video camera is an invaluable tool both for assessment, and to record developments. It provides the opportunity to re-examine events after the session, looking for subtle nuances of behaviour that can easily be missed when working with an individual. Clear examples of the child's communication can be shown to other members of staff, making them aware of specific points to look for themselves when working with that person.

Written records may be required, and unless these can be written later from video evidence they should be kept simple. Within the sensory room the teacher's concentration should be focused on the child's interactions, and responding sensitively to them. Stopping to write notes can affect this, as can the presence of someone else acting as a scribe.

Cause-and-effect work

The term 'interactive environment' is often used to describe the results of the marriage of multi-sensory effects with switch control technology. Much of the initial work in this area used simple controllers that would run any mains appliance, and further developments soon allowed switch control of a complete range of equipment within a room. This encouraged children to act upon their environment by providing a powerful stimulus in response to a simple movement (see Reed and Addis, this volume).

The ultimate aim of any cause-and-effect work is to teach an individual child that s/he can affect his or her environment. The individual can take control to a greater or lesser degree, making personal choices about what s/he wants to see or hear or feel, and exercising a degree of personal autonomy. Switch training is a most important life skill. Indeed, in any home you may use a simple wall switch or dimmer switch to operate lights; you may use infrared switches to operate the television or hi-fi, and switches on timers to turn the video recorder on and off again. As a general part of life skills development all pupils should have opportunities to use such switches, and the multi-sensory room offers a controlled environment with appropriate equipment to provide such experiences.

Interaction

Despite the use of the term 'interactive environments', in reality switch-operated systems can become very far from interactive. The child may be able to control the light, and may react to the light, but the environment and the child may not in any real sense interact. The teacher working with the child must aim to ensure social interaction, with the child responding to the adult or other children. The teacher must remain part of the process.

Case study: Peter

Peter is a pupil in a school for children with severe learning difficulties and although not medically diagnosed, he is considered by the staff to show autistic-like behaviours. He was adept at using a single switch with appropriate software on the computer, and as a progression his teacher moved him to using an interactive light effect with four switches. He soon mastered this, creating sequences of colour, and he also worked out how to change modes on the unit to create his own activities. Again his work was developed further, and he began to operate four major effects in the multi-sensory room with his four switches, the concept of which he grasped with relative ease. Unfortunately, whilst developing switching as a skill, he was withdrawing further and further from social interaction. Providing a switch-operated environment gave Peter the perfect opportunity to retreat further into a private world of powerful images and stimuli.

In one centre for children with autism, all the switches have been placed at a level that is inaccessible to the child, who must use the teacher to operate the switch. In this way the most important aspect of communication – the need for interaction – remains part of the sensory work.

Communication

When communicating with another person an individual is combining a whole range of skills, some physical, some cognitive and some social. In order to help children learn to communicate we must ensure the combined development of these skills. Kiernan et al. (1987) provide a structure for this development that has formed a basis for much of our work in this area. The need to interact comprises both having something to say, and having a reason to communicate.

Case study: Sheila

Sheila was considered by her class teacher to have challenging behaviour. She responded to all equipment by mouthing it, and further intervention resulted in outbursts that culminated in Sheila throwing herself to the floor, where (due to her size and problems of control) she often had to be left. The school had a multi-sensory room, which Sheila's class used for massage and contact relationship sessions. However, as Sheila responded quite negatively to these contact sessions, she tended to sit apart from the group, by the bubble tube or fibre-optics. If either of these were not switched on she would interfere with the group session, walking over the other children and grabbing adults by their clothes or skin. The result would be that her teacher would switch on the equipment to settle Sheila down so they could continue their session undisturbed. As a result of a review of the multi-sensory sessions, it was recognized that Sheila was trying to communicate that there was something that she liked and wanted, and work was developed to provide Sheila with a more acceptable manner of making her request.

Discussion

Sheila recognized that her action could affect the behaviour of other people in specific ways. The concept of cause-and-effect forms the basis of the realization that what you do as an individual can have an effect upon somebody else. Later work with Sheila focused on turn taking. Sheila had begun to interact with her teacher when they sat with the fibre-optics, at first both holding handfuls of the strands but then with Sheila taking strands from the teacher, and passing them back. A switch was introduced, and the teacher would switch off the effect and then pass the switch to Sheila, who would switch it back on. As well as simple turn taking these sessions were developing appropriate social responses. As with Barry, activities in the multi-sensory room helped to promote a more positive attitude between teacher and child. There are numerous ways in which relationships can be formed and developed, through physical contact in contact dance sessions, foot and hand massage sessions or simply in the mutual sharing of experiences so that the teacher does not overpower the child.

Conclusion

The technology used in multi-sensory rooms is still so new that most users are constantly discovering new capabilities of their equipment. Clearly anyone using such an environment must be prepared to adapt and change, in order to maximize the benefit to the children with whom they work. To achieve this versatility time should be set aside for staff to learn how to use the equipment properly themselves. Not simply to switch it on, or programme the switches but to touch it, feel it, explore the effects in every way that is possible. It is not until someone is at home with an effect that they can become flexible in their use of it, and adapt techniques to ensure that targets are met.

In the final analysis, developing work in the multi-sensory room is not simply about understanding the technical aspects of the equipment. It is about the imaginative and constructive way in which you put the various components together. The equipment is far too great an investment to be used simply as a cinema or theatre for people with multiple disabilities. As a tool it can elicit response, motivate movement and change attitudes. It can be used to assist the achievement of targets developed for an individual child, but the system will facilitate developments only where appropriate interaction occurs. No matter how much has been invested in materials and equipment, the most important asset in any multi-sensory room is the individual working with the child. It is their knowledge and skills that will make the room work to earn its investment.

CHAPTER 8

Developing a concept of control

Leighton Reed and Christopher Addis

Introduction

As we become more educated and experienced in evaluating the specific needs of children with multiple difficulties (including multi-sensory impairment), we are increasingly drawn towards 'creating a learning environment' in which children can explore the notion of control. This often involves developing 'acoustically friendly' and 'visually appropriate' areas in which their needs can be adequately addressed.

Some rooms or work areas, for example, may seem very sterile and bare, and when sounds are made they may produce echoes which are particularly upsetting to a hearing aid wearer. This problem can easily be rectified by adding carpets and hanging curtains. This need not be expensive, as simply hanging soft materials or fabric drapes will reduce reflected noise from walls and ceilings. Corrugated cardboard, egg boxes or cork tiles are also good at absorbing sounds or, at the other extreme, commercially produced acoustic tiles are available. Similarly, the visual environment may need adapting so that the right level of visual stimulation is achieved. Some children will respond best in a highly stimulating environment offering lots of bright colours and contrast, and where reflected light and iridescent materials abound. Conversely, some children will find this too much and experience 'sensory overload'. These children will do better in a more controlled environment with far less visual distraction or clutter, where they may focus upon one visual stimulus at a time.

Any adaptations must take account of the fact that we cannot regard these children as a homogeneous group with similar needs and requirements. When considering an 'appropriate' environment we have to consider various combinations of sight and hearing impairment plus any additional social, emotional, physical and intellectual needs the children may have.

This may best be achieved by analyzing what we describe as 'strategies of empowerment'. In this chapter, we describe the working framework which we use when we employ switching systems to pass the locus of control over to a child. Switching systems lend themselves to this aim, and careful consideration needs to be given as to how they may best be utilized within our often contrived learning environment.

What is a switching system?

We want to capitalize upon an arrangement whereby, with a small movement of some part of his or her body, the child can produce a grand rewarding effect. We are prepared to use anything if we are sure that the child enjoys, or is proud of, the result of his or her actions. A well positioned light switch will do, or the keyboard of an electronic organ. In our Unit we have a visually impaired girl who derives wonderful motivation from the noisy warm airflow of our automatic hand dryer. All she has to do is lift her arm a fraction, and it all happens! Indeed, we need not think only in terms of electrical gadgetry. For one little boy, who has limited arm movement and some vision, we stack up a pile of cardboard boxes, painted in bright colours, next to his chair. He squeals with delight when a tiny push sends them crashing down all over the room.

What we are trying to create, then, is an environment in which the child has some degree of control, an environment where s/he can make something nice happen. We want children to understand that they have the power to do things in the world, we want them to understand the idea of cause-and-effect, we want the beginnings of a programme which will help us to improve mobility, cognitive skills and self image.

To create a really flexible learning situation we need something more than the static types of interaction mentioned above. For the purposes of this chapter, we are primarily considering commercially produced switching systems. They can be expensive, but their advantages are many. They allow us to arrange activities which are tailored to the individual needs of each child, and their educational value is enormous.

Educational value of interactive switching activities

- They are based entirely upon what the child enjoys.
- They enable precise programmes to be worked out for the child.
- They allow for accurate assessment of a child's progress, however slight that might be.
- Tasks can be made more challenging or more difficult by degrees.

- Activities can be tailored to meet each child's learning needs.
- They capitalize upon the child's remaining senses and upon the range of his or her physical movement.
- They are absolutely flexible, limited only by the imagination of the teacher or parent.
- They allow the child the chance to make choices.
- The child may develop intentionality through the cause-and-effect nature of the switches.
- If it is felt desirable, a switching setup permits a child to work alone. No youngster really wants an adult at his or her shoulder every moment of the day, and yet the abilities of some children are so restricted that constant adult prompting and motivation may seem necessary. Switching systems can be arranged so that the child enjoys a quality learning activity alone.
- Such programmes can help children to break through the barrier of tactile defensiveness.
- They allow gradual transfer of control to the child.

Before any system is put into operation, the educator must identify its aims – Why is the switching activity being used? What skills or concepts are being worked towards? S/he must also plan how these aims are to be achieved – How will the system be set up initially? How might it be extended as the child learns? These stages are considered in detail in later sections of this chapter.

The switching system

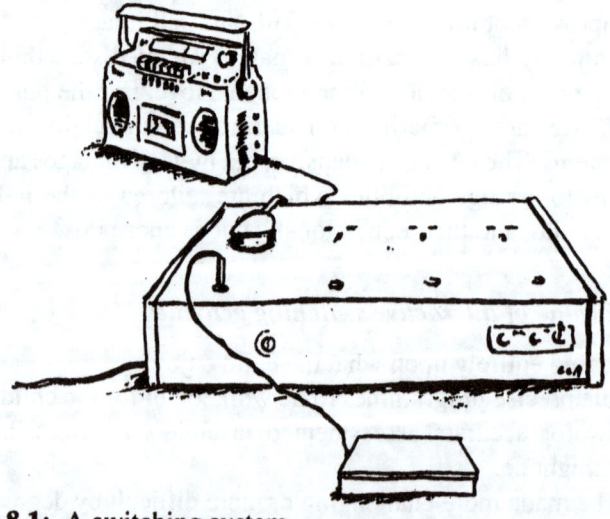

Figure 8.1: A switching system

Figure 8.1 shows a typical switching unit. In this case it is set up so that gentle pressure on the small pad will cause the radio to come on.

Anything that is mains-powered can be plugged into the sockets on top of the system. The jack-plug sockets on the front are for the switches which the child will operate. Switches are usually supplied with fairly long leads, so that the child does not necessarily have to be stationed near the machine. At its simplest, a switch plugged into jack-plug socket Number 1 will, when pressed, switch on whatever is plugged into socket Number 1. For instance, a child lying in the middle of the floor might roll over to touch a pad switch, and at once a string of Christmas lights shines above his head. The next time the child touches the pad switch, the lights will go out again, but the child probably will not want to do this! So the teacher is able to select, from a choice of settings, the one best suited to the needs of the child at that time. Most switching systems offer these basic choices:

- **Momentary:** The equipment comes on when the switch is touched, but goes off again the moment the switch is released.
- **Latched:** When the switch is touched, the equipment comes on. It stays on until the switch is touched again.
- **Delay:** When the switch is touched, the equipment comes on and stays on for a fixed period, perhaps thirty seconds, or two minutes. After this time, the unit will go off on its own, and the child must find the switch again to turn it back on.

Switches

There is a wide variety of switches on the market, some of which we will mention here, and also in later examples of switching systems in use. (It is important to remember that every child presents a unique set of needs – once you have decided which switch to use, it is up to you to offer it to the child in the most useful way. You may need to stick Velcro under the switch, or fix it to a work surface with a G-clamp or with Blu-Tack).

Switches are now available which allow the child to 'switch on' by pressing a pad, pulling a string (rather like a bathroom light switch), squeezing a ball, moving a joystick, placing a hand near a touch sensor, sucking and blowing, pressing a cushion, stepping on a mat, touching a metal plate or squeezing a joystick. There are sound activated switches, eye-blink switches, switches designed for use under ultraviolet light and many others besides. A list of suppliers is given at the end of this section.

(Several of our switches we produced ourselves. Any apparatus where a pair of metal contacts touch together and separate, and are joined by wire to the terminals of a jack plug, will activate the switching system).

Switching systems in practice

Perhaps the best way to demonstrate the advantages of interactive switching systems is to describe a few situations from our own experience.

Figure 8.2: The 'A' frame

1. The A-frame

Peter lies upon a vibro-bed under our tubular A-frame (see Figure 8.2). Loudspeakers and an electric fan are set close to him. An effects projector with rotating moving patterns is mounted on the shelf above him. A string-pull switch is taped to the top of the frame, and connected by string to a hanging yellow wooden rod. The switching unit is set to 'Delay' mode, so that it switches itself off after 14 seconds. Some months ago we used just the one rod – when Peter pulled it, all the rewarding stimuli came on at once. When this became too easy for him, we added a second, green rod, and Peter had to choose. Now we have four rods of different colours. Only the yellow one triggers the switch, and occasionally we move the rods around so that the yellow one is in a different position.

The skills addressed here include fixation, scanning, tracking, directed reaching (including crossing midline), and colour selection.

2. The standing frame

Gemma is in her standing frame. A sensitive pad switch is taped to the end of a piece of wood, which is in turn clamped to the work board of the standing frame. The pad is set in such a position that it is vertical, and only a few millimetres from Gemma's better hand. Eight items from our Unit's stock of mains-powered equipment are plugged into the system – a stereo system (the speakers lie face down on the resonance board under Gemma's frame: she has a profound hearing loss); a projector; a spotlight; two different sets of Christmas lights; a fan; a fibre-optic spray; a vibro-cushion. Her switch is plugged into jack-plug socket Number 1 on the Unit, but here we have chosen one of the additional mode settings provided by the manufacturer. Each time Gemma touches the switch, it moves on to the next one of the eight 'rewards'.

As yet, Gemma is only touching the switch by accident. Every time she does, something new happens. We want her to discover that she is the cause of what is happening. We hope that, eventually, she will seek for the switch with real intention. (Through experience we have found that children learn best if they are allowed to discover for themselves the switch and its effect. We were tempted to keep placing Gemma's hand upon the pad, but from her point of view this is too passive and the rewards are the result of our actions and not hers).

The skills addressed here include the comprehension of cause and effect. As we begin to move the switch further away her directed reaching skills can also be developed.

3. The darkroom

Eight different switches each produce eight different visual effects in the darkroom. The switch mode is set at 'Momentary', so a light goes off immediately pressure upon the switch is released. Switches may be hidden in little boxes, or under cloths, and fluorescent overlays may be attached to switch tops.

The skills addressed here include fixation, scanning, tracking, directed reaching and selection.

Extending the tasks

Naturally, when a child with multi-sensory impairment is first offered a switching system, the action required will be relatively simple. The switch will be arranged in such a way that pressing it is within the current functional abilities of the child. Once the child has mastered this first step, the operator has to consider ways of making the task harder, or more demanding. How this is approached depends upon the nature of the system, the sensory deficits of the child and many other factors.

At this point it is necessary to return to the original questions, asked before the child was given the system – 'What am I doing this for? What particular skill have I decided that the child needs to address and to develop?'. It is very important that switching systems should be regularly evaluated and extended – it would be all too easy to say. 'Look, he can do it, he likes doing it. Let's just leave him alone,' but that would not be in the child's long term interests. The few examples of task extension listed here may help show the progression that must be planned from the very start of the programme:

- 'Shape' the child's behaviour. When s/he finds a switch too easy, move it away slightly. When that becomes easy, move it further. After a while s/he will be reaching for it, or actively seeking it.
- Produce a dummy switch, so that the child must identify the real one by colour, texture, shape or another characteristic. When s/he is successfully 'choosing', add another dummy, and another, or perhaps make the difference between the two less obvious – for example, one large Braille dot on one, two on the other.
- Reduce the number of rewards offered, or change them, so that the child does not become bored or habituated.
- Change the angle of a lever switch to improve wrist action. In fact, make any changes which you consider will shape the child's actions towards the required goal. Do it gradually, and only do it when the previous level of difficulty has been fully mastered.

Prerequisites to employing a switching system

Of key importance is the way that the teacher and others assess, monitor and evaluate children's abilities so that meaningful switching activities can be developed for them. This strategic function cannot be overemphasized since 'getting it right' may well enable the child to develop some of the prerequisites for social interaction. This, for us, involves asking three fundamental questions:

- What form should the assessment take in order to provide an objective baseline of the child's present abilities?
- What types of rewards elicit the best response from the child?
- How can I channel his or her responses in a functional direction?

It is our deliberate intention to place greater emphasis upon 'portable switching systems' than upon commercially produced hardware and software packages. Whilst we are not denying the usefulness of such technology, our experience has led us to believe that it sometimes fails to engage or motivate our children as well as a fan, light or vibration reward linked to a simple switch. This, we suspect, is because simple switching systems are often cognitively more appropriate for our children, and are easily tailored to suit a wide range of environments. For example, the use of an air switch or voice activated switch to blow bubbles in a spa bath provides an effective and powerful reward for some of our children – not easily replicated by a computer!

Baselining – creation of a skills inventory

We need a thorough overview of the child's abilities in all areas before establishing an individual set of switching experiences. One method we have found useful is to suggest that practitioners play 'skills detective', whereby they attempt to deduce the skills their child may need to enhance or develop. This is best done by operating a two tier system of assessment.

The first tier involves collating and analyzing all the available 'objective' clinical data on the child. This is often confidential and one needs to work closely with parents and professionals to gather the required information concerning the child's sensory impairments. Audiologically speaking such assessments may include brain stem evoked response audiometry, evoked oto-acoustic emissions and impedance tympanometry. Similarly, visual assessments may involve viewing the eye with an opthalmoscope (pictures of the retina can also be taken and fluorescein angiogramy can be used to check for abrasions or ulcers) and in some cases electroretinograms may be employed.

The second tier involves baselining the functional abilities of the child. Other more subjective behavioural and distraction-type tests of sight and hearing can also be used at this point to widen the clinical understanding. This must be done in close collaboration with parents and carers, who are often best able to interpret the child's reactions. Some children may in addition have a plethora of reports prepared by physiotherapists, occupational therapists and speech therapists, and these need careful consideration. At the end of this data-collating period we are better prepared to construct a meaningful set of interactive switching tasks for the child, based upon our interpretation and analysis of available and relevant information. We need now to ask the question:

What skills areas are we addressing?

Very crudely, we have attempted to collate a myriad of skills under four main headings: Movement, Looking, Hearing, Touching of these main areas can be further subdivided:

- **Movement:** Directed reaching, cross laterality training, dexterity training. (With certain children this can only be done after consultations with physiotherapists and occupational therapists, so that the correct positioning and seated posture is obtained, and an appropriate switching mechanism selected). Always try to provide the child with the choice to experience interaction in a variety of positions: prone, supine, seated, standing frame etc., since each child has his or her preferred position for certain tasks.
- **Looking:** Fixating, tracking, convergence, scanning, contrast sensitivity.
- **Hearing:** Auditory discrimination, sound localization.
- **Touching:** Tactile awareness, tactile discrimination, touch tolerance.

This skills analysis exercise should focus attention on some of the key prerequisite skills for emerging social interaction. Inextricably linked to the skills assessment is the process of establishing what the child finds motivating and exciting. Many of our pupils have reduced or low motivational drive and we must not underestimate the importance of trying to find out what engages their interest. We need therefore to ask the question:

How do we establish a rewards inventory?

Whilst we are establishing a baseline of abilities, we need also to consider the pleasant experiences we can offer the child – environmental stimuli which may motivate him or her to act in such a way that s/he recreates those experiences. The nature of these stimuli will vary according to the needs and preferences of the child, and the imagination and resources of the teacher or parent. Of course, the object of this chapter is to demonstrate the benefits of those 'pleasurable events' which can be initiated by the touch of a switch, but before we can consider our switching programme we need to delve into every area of sensory stimulation which the child might enjoy – sounds and vibrations, voices, rooms with different acoustic qualities, stationary or mobile lights, smells, movements of air, textures, cuddles, water, flavours, movement, rough and tumble play, activity toys and so on.

We have to know what the child likes, and all children are different. It goes without saying that some children love a footspa whilst others do not. Some children do not want to be held; some hate ice cream; some must not be exposed to rapidly flashing lights. With many children the building up of a 'rewards inventory' is not a difficult task. Indeed, it is a very pleasant one which results in a better knowledge of the child. In the case of some other children it can be very difficult to read pleasure or displeasure or preference in their faces or body movements – for these, the inventory of pleasant experiences can best be established through discussion with all those who know and love and care for the child.

When we come to plan switch-based learning experiences, we discover that some environmental stimuli lend themselves more readily to switching than do others. Most lights come on instantaneously. Smells can be wafted by electric fan, but the effect is not instant. Rough play cannot be earned by pressing a switch. Mother's voice can be recorded on tape, but the three seconds it takes for the tape to 'click in' after it has been switched on may be too long for some children to realize that the sound is the result of their actions.

Below is an example of how a rewards inventory was established for one of our pupils.

Robert came to us at the age of three. He has no vision, has a moderate hearing loss and cannot yet walk. When he arrived he refused to explore, or even touch, objects or textures with his hands. He can laugh or cry to express strong preferences and we are able to read likes and dislikes from his body language and facial expression. His parents are extremely supportive.

It did not take us long to discover an 'ideal world' for Robert – the most blissful, pleasing setting we could produce. He sits in his high chair with his feet in a warm vibrating footspa. Popular music with a good drum beat bombards him from speakers set to either side. An electric fan wafts the scent of eucalyptus over him. He grins wickedly and gurgles with joy. The assessment of what is 'nice' for Robert was not difficult. It was based simply upon a knowledge of his sensory strengths and deficits, discussions with his parents, and much trial and error. Robert likes the vibrating footspa, but no other form of invasive vibration. His parents had done the hard work in discovering his favourite music. We tried one aromatic oil after another in front of the fan, and his choice of expressions made it surprisingly easy for us to identify those scents he liked and those he did not. Now we have somewhere to start from: a mains-powered world of sound, sensation and smell tailored to Robert's own preferences. A switching system may help Robert to learn to control that world.

Establishing home links

How do we attempt the transfer of classroom-based learning into the home or care environment, so that generalizations may occur? This must be the sixty-four thousand dollar question.

It is not easily achieved due in part, our experience suggests, to three main factors:

- The often high staffing ratio afforded to children whilst in school (we use an intervenor model and have a 1:1 staffing ratio).
- The sometimes inappropriate use of switching systems in schools, in that little thought may have been given to the long term rationale of offering a child this form of interaction.
- The fact that switching systems offer an 'artificially contrived' style of interaction.

These factors have the cumulative effect of tipping the odds of successful transfer of skills against parents and carers. They cannot reasonably be expected to mirror the intensive interaction provided by the school, due to the everyday stresses and demands life places upon them, whilst carers in residential homes may have many other children with their own wide agenda of needs.

In addition, some children are offered switching systems without full regard to their possible future effects upon the child's functional skills repertoire. We are not denying the obvious payoffs of lights, projected images etc., for many children. It is not our chosen remit to discuss this less planned interaction. Our concern here is that switching systems are part of a hierarchy, whereby one learned action becomes a prerequisite for a more complex and generalized one. Coupled to this is the fact that switching systems are somewhat artificial – not many children are fortunate enough to have access to switching controllers at home, and not all things in life are switch-operated!

To try to ameliorate these anomalies we have established a two-pronged campaign: the raised awareness of the adult as a switch, and planned intervention.

Parents and carers as switches

In working closely with parents and carers to develop a partnership, we aim to raise their awareness that the cheapest, most cost effective and efficient switches are *themselves*. This is best demonstrated, largely through videotape, by the simple and effective use of mimicry: for example, child vocalizes, adult responds; child moves arm, adult moves arm; or vice versa.

This creates a 'learning cycle' – not something we have invented, but the focus of all quality interaction (see Figure 8.3).

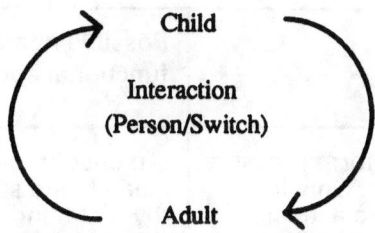

Figure 8.3: Child-adult interaction

Moreover we see our involvement as facilitators, working with the parent or carer to establish the person/switch concept, and offering practical ideas and support. To this end we have found approaches such as aromatherapy and interactive massage (with appropriate training) to be useful vehicles for driving this interaction.

Planned intervention

Planned intervention involves working with physiotherapists and occupational therapists, in particular to try to extrapolate the functional activities which a child will be able to achieve.

Strategies involving switching systems are then instigated to try to assist generalization into functional use in the home/care environment. Table 8.1 gives just a few examples of this approach. Please note that this is not a definitive list and (as with most issues relating to switching systems) the opportunities are limited only by *your* experiences and ability to devise suitable scenarios (and of course the child's own ability level). However, the examples chosen are those which we feel most lend themselves to generalization.

It must be stressed above all that the person directly interacting with the child inevitably becomes the 'expert'. It is the adult's acquired knowledge of the child coupled with the sort of information our working framework provides that facilitates solutions to problems. It has to be borne in mind, however, that one particular switching scenario will not necessarily provide skills generalization. A combination of several different intervention settings may be needed.

School-based switching system	Possible home/residential functional application
'Leaf-type' or Platform pressure. Ideal for athetoids. Only light pressure needed to activate switch. Used horizontally for best results.	To encourage better tactile search and scan techniques by 'flat hand' travel over larger surface areas. Playing of keyboard. To encourage operation of paddle switches on walls to control lights in bedrooms etc.
Lever switch. Operated by very light touch.	To encourage enhanced grip so that door handles be turned or brushes held to comb hair, operate electric wheelchair. Hold finger food, sandwich etc.
Airball Switch and/or Grasp Switch	To encourage self help skills, e.g. pulling trousers up/down, pulling shirt up/down. Squeezing toothpaste out of tube. Operating door handles. To encourage the brushing of teeth, combing of hair. To encourage the pulling up of a zip.
Wrist / Head Mercury Tilt Switch. Attached to limb or head activates when tilted.	Useful for developing head control, directed looking and reaching, and encouraging gross body movements.

Table 8.1: The functional application of swtiches

Conclusion

The importance of switching systems in providing interactive settings for individual children cannot be overemphasized. However, we must never become complacent about the switching environments we create. It is the practitioner's job to try to be one step ahead of the child. Failure to do so may mean that interest will not be sustained, or that the child may become habituated. You must expect constantly to update and modify switching systems to maintain the child's desire to interact. The activities need systematically to increase in complexity in order to provide greater challenge, but in such a way as to avoid secondary problems. For example, increasing the gap between switches may extend a child's directed reaching skills, but may be detrimental if he has too reduced a visual field for such wide visual scanning.

Developing a 'concept of control' for the child is therefore no easy task. It is, we feel, best attempted within a tiered framework which involves:

- Establishing a comprehensive sweep of both clinical and functionally observed data.
- Collating and analyzing the data prior to trying out switching systems.
- Establishing a skills analysis and reward repertoire.
- Extending and generalizing skills and directing them towards a functional usage (wherever possible).

The successful outcome of the work is the raised self image and self esteem the child acquires as a result of being able to effect change, no matter how slight and inconsequential the interaction may appear to the observer.

Switch suppliers

SpaceKraft Ltd., Crowgill House, Rosse Street, Shipley, West Yorkshire, BD18 3SW.

Quest Enabling Design Ltd., Ability House, 242 Gosport Road, Fareham, Hampshire PO16 0SF.

ROMPA, Goyt Side Road, Chesterfield, Derbyshire, S40 2PH.

CHAPTER 9

Integrating the use of technology with other activities

Trevor Watts

Introduction

We have used microelectronic equipment on a daily basis in our unit for children with profound and multiple learning difficulties (PMLD) for over ten years. During that time we have developed and rationalized the use of computers, their peripherals, and independent microelectronic equipment, and have integrated their use into the general educational plans and routines of the children. This has operated on an individual basis for each child, and within an overall scheme and rationale.

The purpose of all educational work is to improve the lives of the children, either immediately or in the longer term. Often, the microtechnology equipment has been the lead equipment in new areas of work with an individual child. At other times it has been the means of generalizing a skill into a broader area of use.

The most intensive work in terms of preparation, intervention, recording and monitoring is conducted at the lowest skill levels, such as visual-motor and cause-effect (see also Reed and Addis this volume). It is equally important to see, and be able to respond to, improvements in child behaviours at higher levels such as leisure and other generalizing situations.

This chapter begins by considering the development and generalization of basic skills through educational programmes involving microelectronic equipment. The stages of planning, carrying out and evaluating such programmes are then considered in detail. The final section considers further applications of such work, and especially the integration of technology-based work with broad educational aims and a range of environments.

Developing and generalizing basic skills

The computer can be used in ways that encourage children's development: there is a high reliance on the equipment in the early stages, but this diminishes until children are able to continue with their newly-learned skills in everyday life. For example, in the initial stages, the link between a switch and a brilliant and/or loud reward can be made extremely obvious in a darkened room, making the learning of cause-effect much easier.

Educational targets include basic visual and fine motor skills, improving vocalizing and signing, encouraging gross motor positioning and movement, and specific skills in grasping and holding. Computer-related equipment allows skills to be broken down into very small steps that are achievable, and that can be learned and practised in controlled situations. The steps and the rewards can be made very obvious and rewarding to the children, and can be tailored precisely to what children need or like. The children can be unhindered by environmental distractions, their own position and bodily discomfort, or other children.

Children learn skills under controlled conditions, and later apply them to useful everyday situations, through generalization of the skills themselves, the equipment, and intrinsic and extrinsic rewards or encouragements. The environment itself can be manipulated, progressing from a distraction-reduced room (darkened, no pictures, plain dark walls) to a normal classroom or home situation, or out in the big wide world. These different environments can be arranged and graded to build up the children's tolerance to distractions. A child's performance will often suffer when distractions are introduced, and without complete control of the environment in the early stages, many skills may never be learned at all.

If a child finds a variety of different auditory and visual effects stimulating and individually motivating, these can be collected together, and used as a particularly powerful motivator in more open situations and with more difficult switches. The teacher's role can vary in form and intensity, and will include the help and encouragement given before activities, and the rewards given afterwards (intrinsic ones from the screen displays or music, extrinsic ones such as praise or a game of something). Instructions, encouragement, demonstrations or physical guidance can be specified and graded into small steps, to be reduced as intrinsic motivation increases. Computer-related work can provide shared experiences for child and teacher which form a basis for interaction (see Bozic and Sherlock this volume).

Taking basic visual attention as an example, we have had varying, but good, rates of success with many children, mainly using the brilliant screen of the computer as the 'lead' activity in broad programmes. We always try to reinforce computer and microelectronic work with other activities. Visual attention work on screen displays might be reinforced by using equipment such as fluorescent toys, glove puppets, carnival masks, torches and light displays, both in individual sessions and in group social sessions. It is thus often impossible to state categorically how much influence the microelectronic aspect has had on a child's progress. The microelectronic sessions, however, are usually the ones that are observed in the greatest detail, which have the greatest level of intervention, the greatest degree of planning and cooperation, and which are the most closely recorded and analyzed. They are the sharp end of much of the work we have done in developing children's visual skills and fine motor skills, learning cause-effect, beginning to enjoy their auditory sense, to use their vision, to begin to control things – because they are motivated to reach and press, to grasp or place, to sit up, or to walk across the room.

As part of a fine motor programme, for example, Ian learned to operate a grip switch that was fitted into a small wooden bar. This was originally connected to screen displays, to toys and mobiles, and to music. He began particularly to like the music, especially 'The Laughing Policeman', and this became the reward for doing other things. The switch was redesigned to be operated more easily, but remounted so that he had to reach progressively further and higher. He learned to reach, to pull himself up to sitting from lying, to tolerate sitting for long periods, to sit without his body splint, and to tolerate standing in a frame, all with the switch (two switches by then, so he had to grip both at once) and music as the reward. With small hand-held electronic rewards, such as a light effects panel, musical cup and spoon, he learned to grasp, to reach, to hold things and to manipulate them, and he began to use such objects in other situations. The music-only rewards became generalized to other rewards, and the working environment extended to include the main areas of the school.

Overview

All work with children with PMLD, whether or not it uses computer-related equipment, may be broken down into four phases:

1. General decisions and goal setting.
2. Preparation for a series of sessions within a programme, and for individual sessions.
3. Intervention and recording.
4. Evaluation.

General decisions and goal setting

This entails a full multi-disciplinary assessment of the child, his or her current skills, immediate needs and future needs. It may involve the parents, nursing and therapy staff, perhaps doctors, the school classroom assistant or nursery nurse, and may be co-ordinated by the teacher, who will attempt to view the child as a whole being, not as a communications blockage, a mobility problem or a feeding difficulty. There may be differing priorities among the staff, and the needs may be parallel or sequential, but it is important that a range of broad aims is agreed and written down, based on the child's perceived and agreed needs. It is vital to offer a broad and balanced, well differentiated curriculum, as well as one that is experiential and child-centred (in other words, based on the child's own needs). This curriculum will show a continuity of aims and progress, and will demonstrate links with the higher targets that are part of the National Curriculum.

When a child's initial needs have been prioritized, they should be written down on a master sheet, in groups of related targets, possible programmes, routines, methods, and progressions. Some of these will involve the computer, or related equipment, and some will not. This decision will be based on which equipment is considered most likely to be beneficial to the child working towards a particular target. A programme will then be set, describing the broad aim, the specific targets, the types of parallel (non-computer) work to be undertaken, and so on.

Preparation

Once a particular aim is decided upon, and the use of microelectronic equipment agreed, the aim is subdivided into goals, each of which is split into small steps. One person is named as the co-ordinator for the programme. S/he will normally conduct most or all of the sessions, and will oversee the non-computer work that parallels it.

A major decision concerns the specific environment in which the child will work: principally whether the work is to be carried out in a darkened room, a closed room, or an open class situation. The choice of environment will depend on the child's initial skill levels and needs, and the aims of the programme. It will in turn affect the recording of progress, and movement from one environment to another will often be a measure of progress in itself.

The overall programme should be described in detail on a master sheet, and the precise method of working, and exact working conditions described. The master sheet may include, for example, which screen displays or toys the child is looking at, or operating; with or without a musical accompaniment (depending whether the child finds music reinforcing or distracting); the style of encouragement, praise and demonstration given by the teacher; the lights, or lack of them; the child's seating position; and the switch type and mode of operation.

If all these points are noted, agreed and adhered to, then it is easier for the child to make progress, and for staff to observe it, record it and maximize it. Progress may be measured by an improvement or generalization in any of the set conditions, and the agreed recording chart will show what kind of progress is expected. There will also be room for comments indicating unexpected directions of progress.

Intervention and recording

Immediately prior to a session, the teacher will set up the room (if the child is working in a withdrawal room) – the lights, curtains, screen, toys, seat, switch, table, recording book, and so on. The computer is arranged so that it is ready to start when the teacher touches the space bar. S/he does this when the child is brought in and has settled down; there is no 'messing about' by the teacher once the child is in the room.

During a session in which specific improvements in the child's skills are aimed for, the teacher may take a passive or active role. In active sessions, when the child needs encouragement by the member of staff, it is often necessary to have two people present (or to simplify the recording process). The help of a nursery nurse is invaluable, either as an observer, or as the person who actually does the intervening/teaching – giving verbal encouragement, physical guidance, tapping the switch or the screen, moving the child's head or hand, giving hand-over-hand prompting, demonstrating the use of the switch, restarting the displays as a reminder to the child, standing behind the screen and shouting, or whatever else is needed. The passive role is one of observing and recording, once the session has begun.

Much of the recording may be conducted by the teacher, by hand, using an observation 'tick sheet', specific recording chart, observation list or comment sheet.

However, a computer can do much of the recording, and this frees the teacher to intervene, or to observe more broadly, as appropriate. If the child is operating a switch, the computer can automatically record for how long the switch is operated, what mode it is in, and how many times the switch is operated. These data can be analysed by the computer to produce graphs of progress, if required. (At the start of the series, the teacher will already have keyed in the other factors – type of switch, stimulus display, environment, staff name, encouragement, and so on.)

Different types of observation charts are used for each type of activity and success criterion. These charts can be very specific for some areas, such as visual attention, learning cause-effect or operating a variety of switches. They can be quite general when a child's preferences, aptitudes and skills are being observed and assessed, or are being reinforced, or generalized to more open working conditions.

Evaluation

Evaluation involves looking at a child's records and discussing them with other staff and parents to get a balanced view of the child's progress, the continued relevance of certain programmes of work, the value of particular sessions, approaches, techniques and equipment, and the most appropriate direction for the child's work to develop in the future.

The evaluation can take place in a number of ways at several levels, for example:

- Did the child succeed in that session with that particular reward, level of encouragement and environment?
- Did s/he succeed for most of the series? How much of the series? If not, why not, and where do we go from here?
- Did s/he succeed when the room lights were switched on?... or when the switch was changed?... or when the reward was changed from a screen display to toys?... or when the sound was turned off?...
- What happened when sessions moved into the open classroom?... or after the summer holiday, illness or weekend?
- How do the high-tech sessions compare with those using normal equipment?
- Do the computer-oriented sessions need to be intensified? or the parallel ones?

The answers to these questions will determine what happens next. After a series of sessions, or a number of consecutive series, the teacher will review the results in conjunction with other related work that the child is doing. It may be decided to go on to the next stage, go back a stage, repeat something, reinforce it, or try a completely different programme for a time.

And so the cycle of readjustment will continue.

Broad areas of use

For a long time, we saw visual-motor development as the central, structured and most direct use of high-technology equipment. However, there are other, wider, almost peripheral uses that were not originally envisaged, but which have become equally important. These often developed almost incidentally, as children were monitored and conditions and results were analysed for reasons and motivations.

The development and generalization of basic skills, discussed above, is one such use. Others include the attempted reduction of challenging behaviours, and the promotion of environmental control and leisure.

The reduction of challenging behaviours

Challenging behaviours include aggression towards others, self-injurious behaviour and extreme withdrawal. I do not think we have ever completely stopped the seriously challenging behaviours of any children permanently, by any distraction or reward method. Microelectronic equipment has, however, provided brief respites from the behaviours, for short periods, at school and at home. These may be for half an hour's respite as a regular routine, or for calming a child when s/he becomes particularly upset, but not as a 'cure' for the root cause of the behaviours.

The idea is to find a greatly motivating stimulus, one that is more powerful than the internal one, and to build up the children's attention to it and the pleasure they derive from it. Computer-related equipment can assemble a collection of stimuli that the child has found rewarding in other work. This could be a tape recording of electronic sounds, classical music, mother's voice, dogs barking, favourite pop music, teacher's voice, especially saying the child's name and asking questions, or nursery rhymes. These can be collected on a single short tape, and played along with screen displays, possibly alternating with electronic toys, flashing mobiles, lights, the large air fan and a vibrator cushion. It is possible to have the screen displays going at the same time as the other stimuli are sequencing, for additional strength of effect. The use of the vibrator and the air blower adds a new dimension to the effect, and can be quite immediately distracting to a distraught child.

The choice of switch can be important (see Reed and Addis this volume); for example, we have used a vertically-mounted grip switch to reduce rocking, a hand-held grip switch to reduce hand-chewing, and an inset lever switch to discourage a child from sliding out of her chair.

Karen, for instance, would scream and moan whilst rocking and clenching her fists very tightly. With switch-controlled music, we found at first that her rocking increased. After extended experimenting and monitoring, we had Karen gripping a small switch, making her more aware of her hands, using gentle classical music instead of pop, and in a darkened room. In these conditions she would become calm in even the worst of her panic attacks. She became more aware of her environs, calmer, and began to use her hands. Eventually, she was able to use the switches, and calm down, in the open activity area.

Pamela would compulsively rock, and destroy whatever she held. It was eventually possible to design a child-proof switch and build it into a bench for her. She became able to operate it easily, did not rock, would often sit with her feet on the switch, and did not wander unsteadily round the room. This only became possible with considerable teacher input in the early stages – for example, physical prompting, changes of the switch and the reward, leisure periods, assistance at home, and a teacher-controlled switch that cut the music off if she rocked.

Environmental control

Microelectronic equipment may help children to do things that would not otherwise be possible for them. These may relate to communication, for example, with pointer boards or 'wants and needs' screens (either scrolling or quartered). Children may learn to control aspects of the environment such as heating, lighting and curtains, or microelecronic equipment may be used to provide a leisure activity by operating such equipment as tape recorders, televisions, videos, computers, slide carousels, toys, train sets and mobiles. In all these areas, technology is providing children with access to control. This is usually through single-touch and multiple switches that are tailored to each child's most reliable movements.

Leisure

The leisure aspect has been extremely important for our children. It has been the most widespread and successful of the wider uses of the equipment. It is not an idle or pointless activity, but purposeful and planned, albeit pursued in a more low-key manner than the more intensive developmental sessions. This activity provides much pleasure for the children, especially if they are able to control the stimulus themselves. Children can have recreational sessions at odd hours and at home.

Recreational sessions are supervised at a relatively low level, and the child sits in a comfortable chair, in the open class situation, with a switch that is easy to use, and with a stimulus that s/he likes. Usually, we have not used the most stimulating rewards, as these are saved for specific sessions with developmental purposes; and we have frequently used leisure activities to develop children's skills and motivation in an unpressured way. Leisure activities may aim to get the children accustomed to a variety of switches, to keep the switch-operating skill generalized; to develop a child's attention span; to generalize the rewards used; to allow children to work in open, distracting environments; to enjoy sounds and pictures, and so on.

The most passive children, perhaps those with deteriorating conditions, are stimulated to keep more alert with their own 'son et lumiere'. For these children, the use of automatic switches is invaluable in providing rewards, and the splitter switch will alternate activities, for variety. Mains adapters allow an even greater variety of sensations, including personalized slide projectors, optikinetic projectors, vibrating cushions, vibrating foot-baths and air blowers.

More able children are encouraged to improve their fine motor skills and attention span, broaden the cause-effect concept, tolerate distractions, stay in one place (if they are liable to wander unsteadily), and take part in social group activities (as around the slide projector, with family and school pictures on the carousel, and one of the more able children operating the special switch). Dawn, for example, was at one time using the child-proof switch to play music, the inset lever switch to operate the slide projector (and she would often vocalize to other children and staff to come and look at her family and pets), a 'sixer' switch with differently textured pads to operate six different activities, and a grip switch connected to the splitter unit to operate three rewards in rotation.

Trevor was virtually blind, and had a neck spasm which brought his head to the right almost all the time. He was immobile and had no reliable control over his limbs. We wanted to provide him with some stimulation for recreation periods, and if we could find something he enjoyed, we wanted to use it as a reward to motivate him to do other things. We followed a sequence of observation and assessment, trying switches that he could knock, or tilt, or rest his hand on; switches in different modes of operation; strong visual rewards, vibration, computer sounds, music and family voices as rewards; work in the withdrawal room; and so on. Gradually, his programme developed to settle on music and family voices combined, as the reward; working in the withdrawal room; and using a head-operated switch. The switch was mounted next to his head, so that normally his head (in neck spasm) was pressed against the switch, but when he moved his head to a forward-facing position, the switch would operate, and the music/voices would start (switch in 'negative mode'). Later developments found that he could succeed just as well with the lights on (because of his limited vision); with other sound rewards (any sound was eventually fine); sometimes with no sound at all (the click of the switch against his head was a stimulant/reward); and in the open activity area with other children around (because he was only concentrating on the closest stimuli).

During recreational sessions, Trevor's head movements to centre increased considerably in frequency, and the total length of time he was relaxed and out of spasm also increased. His spasms reduced; he became more alert; he vocalized and flexed his fingers more; he was happier than at almost any other time when operating his private musical entertainment.

Review

By no means all programmes of work are successful. We have often repeated series several times, restarted them, changed tack, given them a rest for a while, tried different switches or rewards or different environments, and still had little or no progress to show for it. Sometimes we decided we were 'barking up the wrong tree' with the aims or the detailed goals, or that we had gone about it all the wrong way. Sometimes children regress over holiday periods, or during illness; their tastes may change as they mature, or simply through over-exposure; and they are no longer able or willing to operate a particular switch, or don't find the music motivating, or are too interested in all the other things going on around them.

Computer-related work stimulates staff to think carefully about global targets, broad aims and fine goals, small steps; how to organize parallel activities, and how to reinforce and generalize skills once learned on the computer. They need to think about how to intervene, when and why; about what to observe, and what it means; about what to record, and how; about what the records show, and how to interpret them accurately. They need to use feedback to reorganize or redirect programmes of work; to see success and progression, or lack of it; to see where the problem lies, or which factor was the important one in gaining success.

The importance of the teacher's role in the process cannot easily be overestimated. His or her contribution includes work before, during and after each child-computer-teacher interaction. No two players in the process could manage without the third.

Used properly, the computer and related equipment encourage interstaff co-operation, clarity of purpose, and many ways of working towards a range of targets with children who have profound and multiple learning difficulties.

Part 3

Technology as personal tool

CHAPTER 10

Voice output communication aids

Sally Millar and Stuart Aitken

Introduction

Language and communication are particularly important to those who cannot interact directly with the world through all of their senses – in other words, those who are to some extent dependent on other functions to mediate their interaction with the world. The usual method of mediation for blind people, is speech and language. Children with visual impairments who have difficulties acquiring and/or using spoken language thus have a major additional barrier to learning and development, on top of whatever further disabilities they may have.

The purpose of this chapter is to explore and discuss the possible uses of devices and systems which offer an output in spoken language – either through digitized or synthetic speech – instead of, or supplementary to, other forms of output (e.g. screen display, or hard copy printout). Voice output systems can be useful for assessment purposes. They might be used as educational/therapy aids to support the acquisition and development of language and speech in children. Voice output systems might also be used as communication aids, to provide an alternative or augmentative medium of personal communication.

Teachers, therapists and especially parents are understandably loath to dismiss the possibility that a young child may eventually succeed in communicating through oral speech, and so they may feel uncomfortable about introducing augmentative communication at an early stage. In this chapter, we will argue that introducing voice output devices as part of an early intervention programme cannot do any harm and may do much good – whether the child ultimately turns into a speaking child or a child who uses augmentative communication techniques as a primary method of communication.

The acquisition of language in children with visual impairment

Taking a step back – how early will a language or communication disability become recognisable?

The presence of blindness or visual impairment is in itself an indicator of potential developmental language problems. Mills (1988) provides a useful review of the effects congenital blindness has upon the development of language in children who are blind or visually impaired, but have no additional disabilities. There is some research evidence (although it is difficult to compare across studies) to support the conclusion that the following aspects of the development and acquisition of language might be adversely (or at least differently) affected:

- Preverbal communication: smiling; gesture; eye gaze; reciprocal vocalization; mutual focus of attention; nonverbal interaction (e.g. visually-perceived behaviour such as smiling, gesture, eye gaze, mutual focus of attention, reaching, pointing).
- Speech sounds: extended babbling period; perception of speech sounds; articulation of the full range of speech sounds (though not necessarily disordered phonology).
- Early language: age of onset and rate of development; lexical structure; morphology (reflecting the restricted language used by adults to blind children); syntax.
- Semantic: use of language without full understanding (i.e. 'verbalisms'); understanding of 'sighted' words; terms for locational/spatial relations (deictic terms – this, that; here, there); personal pronouns.

Given this range of possibly detrimental effects of blindness, it is a remarkable testament to the resilience of both biological and experiential forces that for the most part congenitally blind children do go on to develop effective speech and language. While there is still much research needed in this area, it is clear that 'lack of vision alone is not *necessarily* the cause of a serious language problem' (Mills, ibid., p.164; italics in the original). Overall, it appears that blindness is compensated for by other channels of information in the development of speech and language.

Nevertheless, speaking blind or visually impaired children may show differences from non-visually impaired children in their patterns of communication in practice. For example, younger children may verbalize little and/or may show echolalia. With older children, the pragmatics of their conversation may well be very different from sighted speakers. They seem to talk more: they may talk incessantly as a way of attracting, maintaining or directing the attention of others; they seem to ask more questions (Erin 1986); they seem to have fewer changes of topic (perhaps because topic is often signalled by eye-contact behaviours); they use reduced and very different nonverbal conversation behaviours; they may have poor turn-taking behaviour.

But what about language and communication in blind or visually impaired children with additional physical, sensory, and/or severe, profound or complex learning difficulties? Do they have the 'other channels' for information reception and processing that they need? Probably not; for a blind or visually impaired child with additional disabilities, all language and communication differences are magnified (Elstner, 1983), in some cases, into major difficulties of interpersonal interaction and of learning.

Wider effects of communication impairment

Having a speech, language or communication impairment is not 'simply' being unable to speak, but has a profound effect on many areas of development.

If the child's experience of the world of people, objects, places and events is already reduced or at least altered due to visual impairment, the communication impaired child's ability to control and interact with that world is severely diminished. Opportunities to explore, to discover objects and activities, to enquire, to participate actively, to play, to make social contacts and relationships, to control others' behaviour, and to learn are all reduced.

We would suggest that in situations of multiple disability, the communication impairment assumes an importance equal to, or even greater than, the visual impairment. But what model of intervention is appropriate? While there are many schedules of development, normative assessments, intervention programmes and learning materials for sighted children learning language, for the blind child there is, candidly, not a lot to go on (for a discussion of these assessment issues see Aitken, 1995).

Are the language difficulties of multiply disabled children the same as those of blind children, only more severe, or are they qualitatively different? Is their communication behaviour like that of speaking blind children or more like that of nonspeaking sighted children? Or different from both? Very little work has so far illuminated these areas, and we have no definite answers here. But we feel these are important questions insofar as they may affect educational intervention strategies.

Teachers working with children with multiple disabilities and visual impairment, in their search for appropriate intervention strategies, may find that more fruitful ideas arise from the new field of Augmentative and

Alternative Communication (AAC) than from the world of 'Visual Impairment' (VI). (Just as, of course, the world of AAC will have much to learn from the world of VI!)

Augmentative and Alternative Communication: what can it offer to visually impaired children?

What do we know?

We know that all children learn language partly by learning about the world. We know that many visually impaired children learn about the world through hearing and touch, more than through sight. Electronic AAC systems can take input through touch and turn it into output that is auditory.

We know that all children learn to communicate by communicating (not by being taught to imitate or to 'master skills'). We know that for children with disabilities, *opportunities* for communication and a *means* of communication must be put in place as early as possible, so that the child does not become a passive 'receiver' of other people's communication, but perceives him- or herself as an active participator in a two-way process.

Experience in the field of AAC tells us that there are no linguistic prerequisites – for example, intact language comprehension, or symbolic understanding – necessary in order to gain benefit at some level from an augmentative communication aid. In fact, quite the reverse is true. Introduction of a voice output aid may stimulate and support the development of intentional communication (acting to create a specific desired effect or goal) and/or of understanding and appropriate use of a signifier or symbol. Baumgart et al. (1990) describe children using vocabulary they didn't really understand, on a communication aid, in order to 'test out' what response it brought (and thus, to enhance their understanding of it). Beukelman and Mirenda (1992) stress: 'Participation is the only prerequisite to communication. Without participation, there is no-one to talk to, nothing to talk about, and no reason to communicate' (p.177).

With very severely multiply disabled children it can be difficult to see how such participation can be achieved. Nonetheless the initial aim of communication intervention is to establish some level of participation, and to enhance opportunities for it to take place.

Communication technology

The obvious contexts for participation for children are familiar play and social routines. Rather than introducing technology as a new 'stand-alone' addition to the daily curriculum, ('Fred's "doing computer" this morning'), ways should be found of integrating technology and its uses into the existing framework of activities, but in such a way that it can add a new dimension to those familiar activities. The 'right kind' of technology is essential.

Cause-effect – social technology or antisocial technology?

Many practitioners' first approach to technology is to set up a switch to operate battery-operated toys – the famous drumming monkey – or brightly coloured pictures on a computer screen. But some children cannot see, do not notice, or are not interested in the antics of such toys or pictures. Others are interested at first, but the novelty soon wears off.

One way of making switch activation more motivating to severely disabled children is to make it a functional way of controlling their environment. Switches, via a 'Mains Switcher' interface can be attached to mains equipment to allow the child to switch on and off devices such as a fan, radio, food-mixer, hair-drier etc. Successes are sometimes short-lived. This may be because technology is being used in a *nonsocial context*.

Instead of being simply a means to establish understanding of 'cause-effect', and to give the child an experience of independent control – both highly valid aims – switch activation is often treated as an end in itself. The devices that switches can control are seen as the child's curriculum, instead of as a means of participation and of access to a wider curriculum. This approach may be seen as limiting the child: many would argue that success in controlling inanimate objects can in fact *reduce* the child's ability to interact and communicate with people. Beukelman and Mirenda (1992) suggest many ways of using single switch technology to enhance participation in a social context. For example, the child operates a battery lorry that 'delivers' crisps or snacks to each child at the table; the child provides the power to turn on a light, or music for pretend play, 'pass the parcel' games and so on, with a partner or in groups.

Similar ways of achieving interaction would be to use a switch to operate a cassette recorder with a 10 second loop tape (like telephone answering machines) which plays and replays a single recorded message. Activating a switch would produce the spoken message 'Come and play with me'.

In other words technology in and of itself is not necessarily helpful. It is *technology used to increase social interaction* (not to replace it!) which should be the major focus with children who have complex multiple impairments.

Type of speech	Digitized speech	Synthetic speech
Description	Ordinary human speech recorded through microphone and stored electronically ('glorified tape recorder').	Speech generated by computer.
Advantages	• Easier to learn how to use. • Quicker to programme. Can have female, male or children's voices, in any language or accent, (or songs, environmental sounds too). • Can sound more 'natural'. • Cheaper.	• Uses less computer memory than digitized speech. • Flexible and open-ended – anything that can be typed in can be spoken out.
Disadvantages	• Quality of reproduction not always adequate for a big or noisy place. • Restricted to a fixed, pre-programmed set of messages. • Can be a nuisance to change the recorded messages; they generally have to be 'recorded over' one by one or in some cases all recorded from scratch again.	• Programming can be complicated. • Speech quality of some synthesizers is not very good. • Good quality speech is expensive (e.g. DECtalk).
Uses	Younger children and early level learners.	Synthesized speech aids may be more suitable with older and more able pupils.

Table 10.1: Comparison between digitized and synthetic speech

Voice output use: the early stages

1. Naming the world

The first stage of use of voice output devices is to provide immediate spoken feedback from the concrete world of things – in other words to provide an auditory representation of the world for children who may not be able to see, touch or feel normally, due to sensory or physical disability, or who are slow to 'make sense' of what they encounter, and might benefit from repetition.

Taction pads

Children who have even a small degree of reach/ touch/ grasp may use 'taction pads' to make objects themselves 'talk'. A taction pad is a slim transparent mat which can be stuck to any object. A single short message can be recorded into its accompanying digitized speech unit (the VoicePal), so that whenever the object with its taction pad is touched, the message speaks out. For example 'This is my cup'; 'Here's the car, brmm brmmm'; 'Mummy's bag'. Almost immediately after the introduction of this basic naming stage, some messages should be changed to include an element of action, or linking the child with the action/object: 'I sit on my chair'; 'I play with the car'.

In the wider AAC field, where concern is more with communication impaired sighted children, the child at this stage of understanding and acquisition of communicative competence is given messages which are not questions or requests (which imply preferences/choices) – that is a higher stage, coming later. Spoken messages are neutral comments, simply describing the world and 'bringing it to life', and interactions arising from this are usually done nonverbally. However, for the visually impaired child with additional impairments it may be that this stage of 'naming the world' needs to be coupled with messages which include requests/questions and other attempts to engage in social interaction. Otherwise the blind child with multiple disabilities, without recourse to nonverbal routes for initiating interaction (eye pointing, shared gaze and so on) may remain passive, not knowing how to interact.

Talking signifiers

A common example of this coupling of 'naming + interaction' is in the use of signifiers or objects of reference. Here the intention is definitely not to encourage a focus on the object per se but on the representational value conveyed by that object. Taction pads have a role with signifiers as they offer multi-sensory channels for understanding. For example, the *feel* of a cup as a signifier for 'I want a drink' can be enhanced with the *spoken* message programmed in the taction pad 'My cup, I want a drink.'

A wealth of literature has paid tribute to the use of signifiers as prompts for enhancing the child's understanding of routine, helping to anticipate what is to happen next in the day. Taction pads provide an additional element of context.

Beyond the naming of objects, and in this stage of using objects to refer to the associated activity, a variety of strategies are open to the teacher/caregiver. Beukelman and Mirenda (1992) suggest that 'touch cues' should routinely accompany spoken words and be given to the child before each step in an activity. The importance of the touch cues for each step being the same each time, with the same cues being agreed across facilitators, is often stressed. The common format – action, pause, action – can be used across many interactive games and songs and, of course, was first advocated in the form of 'resonance activities' by Van Dijk and his co-workers in the 1960's (Van Dijk, 1965).

The advantage, in cognitive terms, of the taction pads is that the spoken message is specific to the object or activity. The association is immediate; the demands upon the child's representational understanding are reduced.

However, not all children with physical difficulties can use taction pads. A physically non-demanding way of providing immediate spoken language feedback at the level of single objects or single simple movements for physically disabled children is to attach real objects or signifiers to the surface of a single switch/single message VOCA (such as the Big Mack, or Say It). Some devices have room for two or four messages – for example, the double Say It, VoiceMate, Cheap Talk. The number of messages that can be produced like this is limited, though, so the next step is to move to larger devices or to scanning (this is discussed below).

Concept development
Taction pads may also be used in the development of concepts and in category formation, which are sometimes areas of difficulty for children with visual impairment, or to provide for the child a means of engaging in 'sorting' games and activities.

2. Interaction and play

Using technology to enhance participation in play and interaction involves the introduction of functions of language above and beyond the basic identification of objects and activities by name (see Bozic and Sherlock this volume). While naming is an important early stage, a working vocabulary composed only of nouns means that all the child can do is answer questions, which is an abnormal and 'test-like' situation. Additional messages will be needed which include requests, questions, commands, expressions of feeling, and 'regulatory' uses of language to allow strategic and social communication, and imaginative use of language for pretend play etc.

Direct selection of interactive messages
Such messages can be made available to the child who has the hand function to press a flat surface or overlay keyboard. Small sized signifiers can be attached to the square spaces on the top of a multiple message VOCA (usually 4, 8, 16, or 32 squares available). Suitable devices for use of this sort would include the AlphaTalker, Digivox, IntroTalker, Macaw, Message Mate, ORAC, or Speak Easy (see Table 10.2). These are all relatively small and portable, so may be easily integrated with daily activities in different parts of the room, and with different materials, unlike a concept keyboard on a classroom computer.

The child will only have, at first, a very small number of messages, so the choice of vocabulary is very important. At this stage, it is useful to think of vocabulary choices as *topic-specific*. So, for example, a situation with stacking bricks might involve messages like 'Mandy knock them down'; 'You build it up high'; 'It's my turn'; 'I found it'. Very likely, the VOCA will need to be reprogrammed and have the overlay changed, between different activities, rather than always keeping to the same few messages and expecting them to cover every possible communication situation (it's impossible). The principle here is that it may be better to have a few messages that are *exactly* right, for some specific occasion, than to have a few messages all the time that are slightly wrong for *every* situation.

More general messages, if they are used, need to be meaningful (relevant), motivating (preferably funny) and interactive. This does *not* mean messages that say 'I need to go to the toilet'! Instead, it means messages like 'I need crisps!'; 'Hurry up!' 'It's my turn now!'; 'More please!'; 'Stop please, I've had enough'; 'No, no, no!' and suchlike.

If there is some doubt about which message was really intended, prompting/checking behaviours can be developed (and standardized across all communication partners) such as 'You said "Stop now"'; 'Did you mean that?' (wait for yes/no); double-check – 'Do you want to stop now?' (wait for yes/no); If no, 'Do you want to say something else, then?'

Case study

Bobby, a six year old with cerebral palsy and visual impairment, was introduced to an IntroTalker with digitized speech. At first it was used as part of a routine and meaningful activity that he understood well (mid-morning snack time) with topic-specific vocabulary in it. Real objects and parts of real objects were attached to the Talker's overlay. He could feel – and in some cases hear – these before pressing the square underneath (e.g. a rustling crisp bag covered part of the device with the message 'Can I have a crisp?'; a real biscuit meant 'Can I have a biscuit?'). Pressing the crisp bag resulted in him immediately being given a crisp. This highly prompted routine showed that:

- He was very responsive to the voice output.
- He was enthusiastic and motivated to keep trying to feel the interface and press for a message.
- He made the connection between his pressing, the spoken message and the reward (already a three stage operation, rather than a two stage operation such as switch and toy play).
- His accuracy and efficiency in pressing the target area improved.
- He recognized the real objects felt on the overlay.

Overlays and topic-specific vocabulary were swapped as appropriate to different activities and games in the classroom. This approach increased the physical and mental distance between actual objects/ activities and their representation, and added the use of language to otherwise passive or closed 'yes/no' choice situations. Moreover, that language was under Bobby's control, rather than under the adult's control.

3. Making choices

Having understood that objects, with their associated messages, can signify other objects, people, and activities, the child is ready to tell other people his or her decisions about which object or activity s/he wants. This is an important step to independent communication; VOCAs can reinforce this process powerfully by ensuring that choices are unambiguous and responses immediate.

What choices?

Choice messages should be child-centred, fun, interactive and deliverable. For example 'Tickle me!'; 'Soft play, please'; 'Music tapes please'; 'Orange juice, quick!'

Taction Pads may be used again (at a more advanced level this time), to 'label' items in a play shop, or to 'read out' the title of different story books or cassette tapes, so that the child can choose independently what s/he wants to listen to.

What's the pay-off for the child?
The first principle of choice making – on or off technology – is that if children make a choice, they are rewarded immediately by having their message repeated, then being given, or doing, whatever it was that they chose. Therefore, it is important not to display choices which cannot realistically be 'delivered' immediately. If children do attempt to choose but are fobbed off with 'Oh yes, we'll be going swimming next Wednesday'; or 'You'll get a drink after dinner', even the most severely disabled children quickly learn that this was not a 'true choice' but an empty exercise with no apparent pay-off for them, and they will stop co-operating with the activity.

All of the child's possible communication partners require training in the appropriate response to make when the child succeeds in pressing a message. *Inappropriate* responses include things like:

Isn't it wonderful, how that machine talks!

He says he wants crisps but there's still twenty minutes to snack time.

He's not supposed to know that message yet.

Having gained familiarity with the process of choosing between a few activities and objects by the 'feel' of the actual objects or of signifiers, or by their location on an overlay, the next step for the child would be to move to ever wider ranges of choices. Problems! Firstly, it may be physically impossible to 'display' a large number of possible choices in front of the child in concrete form (a visually impaired child may not be able to remember all of what was on offer, anyway). Secondly, what if the choices are of abstract things or actions which are difficult to symbolize in a tactile form? How is a child with limited physical abilities going to recognize and access a larger number of choices?

Access to VOCAs
Learners who have good or even moderately good hand control can directly press the surface of a VOCA to produce the underlying spoken message. For users with poor hand control, many voice output devices incorporate options to allow operation by special inputs such as encoding (reasonable cognitive abilities needed) or scan and switch (reasonable

visual abilities needed). Learners with a combination of severe visual impairment in conjunction with severe physical impairment – and perhaps learning difficulties – are in a Catch 22 position; VOCAs which offer a range of viable selection techniques for such learners are few in number.

Information technology solutions which may be appropriate for blind children may not be at all helpful for multiply disabled children. Even if literacy is a possibility – and often it is not – Braille writing, for example, requires various combinations of finger presses, and so too does the production of Moon symbols. Touch typing with a standard keyboard, though physically less difficult, may still be beyond the pupil's physical abilities. And for the communication impaired blind learner with poor hand function, signifiers and other tactile materials are not useful, nor are graphic symbols.

Switching and scanning remains an option for physically disabled learners, but presents much more difficulty when the child is also blind, as scanning has to be through the auditory medium.

Case study – auditory scanning

Mark (six years) has a degenerative metabolic disorder. His sight has been described as short sighted with an intermittent squint. However, he finds it difficult to use his vision because it takes a long time for him to process what he sees. In contrast, he listens to and understands well most of what is said to him. But he could not contribute to the discussion, initiate communication, or comment on what was happening in the classroom. Because of this, people underestimated Mark's abilities. A VOCA would help, but he could not feel its overlay or press it because of extremely limited hand movement.

An appropriate single switch site was identified and a light pressure 'jelly bean' switch in a contrasting colour was used. Mark quickly showed he could understand that different switch access modes could be used to operate lights, the TV, and other mains-operated devices, as well as battery-operated toys. The focus of the assessment turned to his communication.

Of the available VOCAs, only the AlphaTalker could be programmed to work in auditory scanning mode. The process involved:

1. Asking his mother what activities motivated Mark. These were
   a) symbolic play – *'I'm Sandy the baby'*;
   b) a school dinosaur project – *'Plesiosaurus will not bite'*; and

      c) a generic phrase that gave him control over events – *'I'm going to have a turn now'*.
2. These phrases were recorded into the AlphaTalker.
3. A 'verbal prompt' (in the form of a keyword) was recorded, attached to each phrase.
4. Mark listened as the VOCA spoke each keyword. At the one he wanted, Mark would activate his single switch and the full phrase underlying the prompt would be spoken out.

For this child, auditory scanning was more effective than visual scanning. Even though Mark had useful vision, it required a great visual processing effort to interpret moving objects and events. A teacher might be misled into thinking that a visual scanning mode would be helpful, when in fact listening may be easier.

If a child can operate an auditory scanning system, they may progress to a more extensive message set. Some communication aid systems offer 'pre-programmed' vocabulary application packages with the intention of removing much of the hard work in creating a symbol, vocabulary and storage system from scratch. However, a serious question is whether the symbology and message content of these packages are appropriate to children who are visually impaired.

4. *Teaching formal language structures*

If a child has progressed through the stages of making choices and physically accessing a device, it may be relevant to consider whether s/he could go on to build sentences from separate words and phrases on a VOCA. For example, instead of producing a whole message with one switch press, choosing from a range of subjects (Mum; the boy); verbs (wants; eats) and objects (biscuits; a story) to create new utterances.

At this stage, it might be helpful to use a classroom computer with a voice synthesizer attached, and 'talking' educational software such as Touch Explorer, SoundBook, or Using Symbols, rather than a portable VOCA. The access method might be a concept keyboard or a switch and scan system. Usually, such systems rely on a visual interface (concept keyboard overlay or screen display with symbols or words displayed), but, for a visually impaired child, symbols (even if they are visible) may not be meaningful. The challenge for the next generation of AAC systems is to identify interfaces which do work with the blind child. These might be based on location, or sound, rather than on visual concepts or alphabetic codes.

Conclusion

A range of voice output devices have been mentioned here (see Table 10.2); each has slightly different features, and new hardware and software is coming out all the time. Voice output devices may be thought of as tools to be used for specific tasks, not necessarily as permanent aids which the child must use at all times, to the exclusion of other materials. As discussed in detail by Fisher and Thursfield (this volume), careful assessment of the child's needs and abilities is very important.

Although the design of voice output devices makes them increasingly simple to manage technically, finding effective ways of implementing them and integrating their use into a child's individual educational programme is not at all simple. Support will be available from other professionals, however. With input from specialists in augmentative communication, speech and language therapists, and teachers of the visually impaired, teachers will be able to piece together a working package of special techniques and new technology to enhance the communication opportunities of children with multiple disabilities and visual impairments.

Further reading

Light, J. (1989) 'Towards a definition of communicative competence for individuals using Augmentative and Alternative Communication Systems', *Augmentative and Alternative Communication,* 5(2).

Rowland, C. (1983) 'Patterns of interaction between three blind infants and their mothers'. In Mills, A. (ed.) *Language Acquisition in the Blind Child: Normal and Deficient.* London: Croom-Helm.

Schweigart, P. (1989) 'Use of microswitch technology to facilitate social contingency awareness as a basis for early communication skills', *Augmentative and Alternative Communication,* 5(3).

Device	Company/Address	Price Guide (approx.)
AlphaTalker	Liberator Ltd., Whitegates, Swinstead, Lincs. NG33 4PA. Tel. 01476 550391 Fax 01476 550357	£1295
Big Mack	Liberator Ltd.	£93
Cheap Talk 8	Toys for Special Children – Enabling Devices, 385 Warburton Ave., Hastings-on-Hudson, NY 10706, USA. Tel. 914 478 0960 Fax 914 478 7030	$120
Digivox	Dynamic Abilities, The Coach House, 134 Purewell, Christchurch, Dorset BH23 1EU Tel. 01202 481818 Fax. 01202 476688	£1695
IntroTalker (refurbished only)	Liberator Ltd.	£649
Liberator	Liberator Ltd.	£5795
Macaw	Toby Churchill Ltd., 20 Panton Str., Cambridge CB2 1HP Tel. 01223 316117 Fax 01223 462037	£899
MessageMate 20/40	Cambridge Adaptive Communication, The Mount, Toft, Cambridge CB3 7RL Tel. 01223 264244 Fax 01223 264254	£425

ORAC	Mardis, Business Development Centre, Fylde Ave., Lancaster University, Lancaster LA1 4YR Tel. 01524 593692 Fax 01524 848123	£930
Say It (single) Say It (double)	Toys for Special Children – Enabling Devices	$55 $65
SpeakEasy	Liberator Ltd.	£399
Taction Pads (set of 5)	Quest Enabling Designs Ltd., Ability House, 242 Gosport Rd., Fareham, Hampshire PO16 OSS Tel. 01329 828444 Fax 01329 828800	£56
VoicePal Plus	Quest Enabling Designs Ltd.	£491
VoiceMate	Cambridge Adaptive Communication	£255

Table 10.2: Suppliers of Voice Output Communication Aids

CHAPTER 11
Augmentative communication

Dithe Fisher and Clive Thursfield

Introduction

In this chapter we describe an approach to assessment in the field of alternative and augmentative communication, and illustrate how the approach has been applied in some very diverse cases. We characterize our approach as *structured*, and contrast it with alternative assessment approaches characterized as *ad hoc*. We argue that whilst a structured approach requires more initial effort, it may avoid some potential pitfalls which make the ad hoc approach less effective in the long term.

We use the term 'assessment' to encompass a process of evaluation and intervention which ultimately leads to the establishment of an appropriate, effective communication system. For the practitioner, the process has two aspects: thinking, and doing. Both are crucial. The process is cyclical: a pattern of evaluation, planning, active intervention and re-evaluation leading to further planning and intervention until the goal is reached. This requires an extended period of time.

Such a process need not necessarily involve a specialist centre like our own. It should be possible to apply the principles of structured assessment at a local level. Indeed, many people have good communication systems developed with local input only. Unfortunately, things have not always gone so well, for various reasons. Compared with typical local practices, our approach may appear time consuming. There is often only one chance to get it right; we cannot risk wasting this chance by setting off without a clear, rational plan.

Basic philosophy

Whilst each assessment is unique we have evolved a general procedure which helps us tackle each new situation systematically. As we describe this process in detail, we hope to show how the practice stems from our underlying philosophy, and how the procedure enables us to piece together all the information necessary for effective planning.

Our involvement begins with a one or two day first assessment which takes place at the centre, unless the child is unfit to travel. *A communication problem does not belong to the child alone; it also belongs to all those who have significant contact with that child.* We therefore encourage family, school staff, and other professionals to attend the initial assessment. A typical team might include six people, but there may be twice as many. It may appear impractical to ask so many people to travel to the centre, to meet with our smaller team, but a special focus, such as assessment at a specialist centre, may be needed before everyone makes the necessary time commitment. This is sometimes the first time all the significant people have met together. Teams often say how valuable it is to meet and spend this time focusing on one child. Another advantage of meeting outside the regular environment is that team members cannot be called away unexpectedly, to join another child's review, or to cover for staff sickness.

Initial assessment process

Once everyone has arrived, we welcome them into the assessment room and offer refreshments. We then explain the overall assessment process. We explain that the initial assessment is just a start: our first chance to get to know the child and the team, and to plan the first steps. The overall assessment is likely to involve a series of meetings, each followed by a programme of actions and a further review, until we and/or they feel we have gone far enough. Parents are often relieved to find that it will not be disastrous if the child does not perform on the day, though they may be disappointed to be advised not to expect to go home with a complete solution on this occasion. We also explain that we work towards person-centred holistic rehabilitation and that, although communication is our primary focus, related issues such as mobility, posture, benefits, education, environmental control etc. form essential parts of the whole picture. We therefore encourage those present to identify any such areas of difficulty and we take steps to begin to resolve them by, for instance, referral to other departments of the Regional Rehabilitation Centre or to local services.

During the initial day(s), the first stage is to ask everyone in turn what they hope or expect from the assessment. Next, in order to get to know the child as quickly as possible, we ask the group to describe the child's average day. In fact the success of assessment may depend on individuals stating their opinions honestly, even if they conflict with what other people say. This stage takes quite a while, as we tease out information about all aspects of the child and his or her life. If the child gets restless we try to provide entertainment without disrupting the discussion, and promise that s/he will be busy in the afternoon. Once we have a good picture of the current situation, and of what has already been tried, we stop for lunchbreak.

The centre team talk through what they have heard and observed, and plan the afternoon's activities over lunchtime. There is no set structure for the afternoon. There will certainly be practical activities for the child. If s/he already uses a switch, computer or communication aid, we may ask for a demonstration. We will probably want to look at how s/he can best access technology, and observe his or her reactions to some of the equipment available. Some of the local group will work with the child, others may be drawn aside for further discussion, whilst continuing to observe through the one-way mirror. Discussions may move on to how to apply and develop what has been seen at the centre, at home and in school.

At the end of the session, everyone gathers together again. The centre team summarize what they have done, and why. We invite the local group to comment on what the child has achieved, and share our own opinions about what has been discovered. Having established a picture of the child's current abilities, needs and opportunities, we have an idea of what might be a realistic long term aim. We now propose a series of short term goals and, if the group agree, specify how these will be carried out. Any actions to be undertaken by our centre will be formally recorded on the Action sheet. Any actions to be carried out by the local team will be described in full in the assessment report. There is no obligation to have further involvement with our centre, but the suggestion of another visit to review progress and plan the next step is usually welcomed. A review date six weeks hence will normally be allocated, but, if this is too soon, we find a more appropriate date. Finally, we need to check that we are working in the right direction. We will ask, 'Have we missed out anything you hoped we would do? Are you unhappy about any of the things we have done? Are we beginning to meet your expectations?'

As we have explained, the assessment process is longitudinal, and will probably involve a number of revisits. There will be other chances to work directly with the child. The initial assessment is a unique opportunity to gain insight into the worlds of the individual and his or her team.

Review

At review, the team compare the actual outcome with the goal. If the goal has been reached, they check that the next goal is still appropriate, and plan how to achieve it. If the goal has not been reached, they examine what has happened. Was the plan carried out as agreed? Did all the equipment work as it should? Were there unexpected disruptions; illness, staff absence, family troubles? If there is no obvious external problem, perhaps the step was too ambitious; could it be broken down further? This cycle of goal setting, intervention and review continues until a satisfactory end is reached. At the outset, it may not be possible to identify specific long-term goals. Our philosophy is, *'Go as far as you can see; when you get there you will be able to see further.'*

Resolving conflicts of opinion

When asked what they expect most people say they want the child to be able to communicate. Depending on the child, they may mean basic control of the environment or, at the other extreme, the ability to exchange information with another person. Within the group, there may be significant differences in expectations, reflecting discrepancies in perceptions of the child's ability and potential. If these are not addressed, the group will not be able to work as a team.

Katy, a multiply disabled and visually impaired four year old, was a typical example. Her parents declared her intellectually normal; school staff believed she had severe intellectual limitations, as well as physical disability. Parents see more of the child, know her history, and may well recognize signals and signs undetected by the school, On the other hand, they also have a lot invested in the child. It is hard enough to cope with a child with special needs; to acknowledge that the child has only limited awareness and ability to respond might be unbearable. In such a situation, we have responsibilities to both child and parents. If we find that the child is functioning at a very early developmental level, it would be unfair or even dangerous to set up a system which appeared to allow her to communicate more sophisticated ideas. We should try to guide parents towards more realistic expectations, whilst offering positive suggestions about what the child can do now and what technology may enable her to do in future.

Graham's parents were in no doubt that he had learning difficulties. However, media coverage of technology for people with special needs had convinced them that, if only Graham could be given the right device, he would be able to express all the thoughts that must surely be locked inside. Certainly, there would be very positive ways that Graham could use a communication device to take more control over his life, but this might fall short of the transformation his parents had in mind. We had to explain that whilst technology can open doors, it can only let out what is inside. Sadly, they found this hard to accept and so, despite Graham's successes, they ended up feeling disappointed.

Occasionally, parents expect less than other participants. Stuart was the youngest child of a large family who all doted on him. No one at home expected him to be able to do anything independently. The physiotherapist had noticed that he did a lot more for himself at school, but she had never shared this observation before. We encouraged her to talk about it with Stuart's mother. If she never demanded anything from him, Stuart would naturally take the lazy option, reinforcing her belief that he was physically unable to help himself.

Sadly, some carers have acquired low expectations because of poor service provided by other agencies. They want the child to be assessed to be sure they have done all they can, but will not be surprised if there is nothing suitable. How have they reached this point? Countless disappointments and delays; equipment taking so long to make that the child has outgrown it before delivery; placements which appear to imply permanent total dependency. To avoid further disappointment, carers may protect themselves by expecting nothing. Happily, carers are generally so excited by what they see the child achieve during the assessment, that they readily adopt more optimistic expectations. In the rare event that they do not, we might have to focus intervention in the school environment initially, so that the child's progress will not be blocked by negative attitudes.

Facilitating a critical analysis of need

What do we learn from the description of an average day ? We find this a very effective vehicle for gleaning information on all aspects of the child, his or her situation and the attitudes of group members. The structure also seems to work well for the family and other participants. As they describe the familiar daily routine, people begin to relax, and the discussion starts to flow. The parents usually begin, describing the home and the child's morning routine. The teacher, or classroom assistant, takes up the narrative when s/he gets to school, and other participants describe their role at the appropriate point. We try to keep close to chronological order. We warn the group that we will keep interrupting to ask for more detail, and that some questions may appear irrelevant or even nosy! The aim is to explore all the contexts of interaction; what does s/he communicate about? how successful is this? when do breakdowns occur? what does the child not communicate that s/he or others might wish? Are there significant differences in performance between environments, or with different listeners?

Mike's teacher, for example, was astonished to hear his mother's description of the home routine. At school, Mike (aged eight) seemed hard to motivate, silent and generally content to sit and watch from the sidelines. Cognitively, he could only cope with the earliest prereading activities. At home he apparently 'never shut up', was keen to be included in everything, and loved his 'homework'; eye-pointing to flashcards with written words. Delving further revealed that he had been unhappy since transferring from (supported) mainstream infants two years before. At home, he was surrounded by lively and responsive children. His new school class were nearly all nonverbal so the whole environment was probably less rewarding. Our first step was to encourage the school to create opportunities for Mike to integrate with more able children. There would be little point developing a communication system if he would not be motivated to use it.

The daily routine gives clues about the child's personality. If s/he is said to enjoy an activity, we try to tease out exactly what s/he likes about it. Knowing what excites and motivates the child helps design activities to explore or develop his or her abilities; or give more control over those activities, just for fun. An important part of the evaluation of technology is to be able to try it out in 'real life' situations. We therefore routinely loan any aids/equipment for a period of home use.

Karen's helper said she loved wheelchair dancing, especially to the tune of the 'Gay Gordons'. Later, when we were struggling to identify a reliable switching action, we needed to motivate her to keep trying to operate the switch, but she seemed to lose interest in every activity after a couple of tries. Finally, in desperation, we decided to try 'country dancing'. The switch was linked both to the mobility platform and to a cassette player, so that each activation resulted in a few seconds of music and movement. This arrangement proved highly motivating, if rather exhausting for the helper who danced alongside!

Reviewing the routine from morning till night, noting any daily variations, is an effective way of ensuring that no vital information is missed. For example, we may learn that the child is already following a programme recommended by another centre. If the day is too structured to allow any choice-making, and the child is a passive recipient of the activities, this conflicts with our involvement, so we need to know how much flexibility is possible.

What does the *child* need?

The local team may have stated that their expectation is for the child to be able to communicate, but when we ask if there are ever times when listeners do not understand what the child is trying to tell them, or if there is anything the child would like to communicate, we may find that there are currently no unmet communication needs. Sometimes it is the family and professionals who are frustrated, rather than the child. In this situation, we can consider deliberately creating a need to communicate, either by disrupting the existing routine, or by offering new communication opportunities (see also Bozic and Sherlock, this volume).

The first approach is most appropriate for promoting communication of basic needs; when the child is hungry, uncomfortable, wants attention. Many of the children we see are largely dependent on others to meet these needs. Carers are often so familiar with the child that they recognize and address needs before the child has signalled them. It may be necessary for them to hold back to leave space for the child to signal that s/he has a need. We recognize that this can add stress to a routine which is already very full. There are also ethical issues; if the child's current quality of life is good, can we justify making life less comfortable, in order to develop very basic communication? There is no universal answer; each child must be considered individually.

Most human communication is motivated by more sophisticated needs. For example, we communicate to give information, to make others laugh, to assert ourselves. A child who has never been able to use communication for these functions is unlikely to be aware of this as an unmet need. We may look for communication opportunities within his or her daily routine; times when s/he might value being able to convey a message, even though s/he does not attempt to do so now, and may not even recognize that this is possible. We can then provide the means for the child to experience telling a joke, or asking a question, for example. Once s/he has had the experience, we may have developed a communication need where no need existed before, and must recognize a responsibility to find a way to meet this need (see also, Millar and Aitken, this volume).

Assad suffered brain injury at the age of seven. Three years later he had recovered some motor skills, but was still unable to walk or speak. His parents tried to make sure that Assad got everything he wanted, and more. Unfortunately, this had two negative effects: Assad became lazy and passive, and his younger brother became jealous. The poor relationship between the brothers was a source of tension. Assad would shout when young Naheem came too close, knowing that his brother would always get the blame. Naheem called Assad names when no one seemed to be listening, but otherwise avoided having anything to do with him.

In this situation, we saw both need and opportunity. The opportunity was that Assad did initiate communication with his brother although only by shouting, whereas in most situations he would wait passively for the other person to talk to him. The need was for Assad to be able to express messages which would make Naheem want to continue the interaction.

As an introduction, we set up a single switch linear scan on a digitized speech output device with eight locations – each having a cheeky comment, chosen to amuse or provoke a response, rather than cause offence! The scan was set at its fastest rate, and the display turned away from Assad. The idea was that each time Assad operated the switch, one of the messages would be spoken immediately. The random element made the activity more fun. Naheem proved a great ally in this project. He responded vigorously to remarks such as 'You've got a nose like a squashed tomato!', encouraging Assad to press the switch again and again to keep up a stream of insult and counter-insult. When the messages began to lose impact, Naheem invented and recorded a new set. By this time, Assad was ready to move on, and we began to introduce the option of choosing a specific message.

The intervention plan

By the end of the assessment or re-assessment we should have a clear view on the existing level of skill in relevant areas. If as a group we have been able to agree on a set of realistic short and long term aims, it should be possible to identify which skills need to be developed, in which order of priority. The next stage, then, is to work out a programme of activities to develop those skills.

Professionals in alternative and augmentative communication have moved away from the belief that an individual must have certain prerequisite skills before s/he can benefit from an electronic communication device. Some people now even suggest that actually using a device may be the most effective way for an individual to develop those skills. Whilst we welcome the philosophy that there should be no prejudice about who may benefit from technology, we prefer to identify specific subskills to be developed, and select the most effective and practical way to work on each one individually.

Using a communication device generally demands the application of a number of skills at the same time: switching, visual attention, memory etc. If a child needs to develop in all these areas, it might appear logical to use a communication aid so that s/he can practise them all at the same time. There are disadvantages, however. It may not be possible to set up a device so that the demands it presents are at the appropriate level in all areas. Even if this were possible, the child might not be able to perform at his or her best level in a skill which must be combined with other new skills. If s/he does not succeed, we may not be able to isolate the cause or causes of failure. For all these reasons, we generally look for activities where the skills required are well within the child's abilities in all areas except the target skill. We can then monitor progress with the new skill, and if this does not develop as expected, we can usually see what needs to be changed. Such activities may use a wide range of equipment, both high and low tech.

During the initial one or two day assessment it is essential to be able to provide technical and engineering solutions and options quickly, to move through a range of ideas. We need to be able to fabricate special switching arrangements and respond to skills and difficulties as they appear. It may, for instance be necessary to produce an orthosis which contains an infrared switch positioned to utilize the smallest of movements. This may then reveal the need for special electronic conditioning of the switch signal. All these things must be available within the context of the assessment session.

Bridget is a nonspeaking twelve year old with athetoid cerebral palsy and learning difficulties. For two years her school team had struggled unsuccessfully to get Bridget to use an Orac communication aid. They were convinced that access was the core of the problem, and that all they needed was help to find an appropriate switch action.

Certainly, Bridget's switching arrangement could be improved, and with our engineering facilities this was relatively simple. However, when we connected the switch to the Orac, it soon became clear that there were other issues to be addressed. The previous switch action had been so difficult that Bridget could only operate the switch occasionally, with considerable verbal and physical prompting. Now that it was easy to use the switch, a new pattern appeared, with Bridget operating the switch over and over again. This was a positive development, in some ways, but it raised questions: was she operating the switch deliberately, or was it operated involuntarily by athetoid movements? Was she physically able to refrain from switching? Did she understand what the switch was for? Perhaps the problem with switching had overshadowed the possibility that other necessary skills might also be lacking.

With the school team, we now identified skills to be investigated, and set up a programme to look at each in isolation. The information brought back to the next review clarified which skills were already present, and which needed further development. Bridget did have the concept of cause-and-effect but needed to develop switch control and visual attention. We needed to design an activity where she would get a reward if she operated the switch a few times, and then stopped. Bridget's greatest motivation was social interaction, so ideally the activity needed to involve other members of the class.

An Alphatalker was set up with a single switch step scan, and four locations. Each time Bridget pressed her switch, a message was spoken. For variety, a number of message sets were suggested, each following the same pattern. The first two messages were neutral or nonsense (e.g. 'Hello'); the next was a request for a positive event (e.g. 'Chocolate please'); the fourth message negated the request (e.g. 'I don't want chocolate'). If Bridget stopped after the positive message, her partner would carry out the request. However, if she pressed the switch again before they could respond, the request was cancelled, and she had to start again. Our plan used a sophisticated communication device, but we stressed that the device was used to train a specific skill, not as a communication aid in its own right. In fact the device was positioned out of sight to make it clear to staff that Bridget should not be asked to look at the display. All she needed to do was operate the switch.

Introducing a communication device

Once the relevant skills are sufficiently developed, the time finally comes to introduce a communication device. We do this in three broad stages, and make sure that the child has succeeded at each stage before moving on. Depending on the child, it may take days or years to complete the third stage. We try to control the level of risk so that s/he is always challenged, but unlikely to fail.

In the first stage, the child learns to operate the device. There may be an interactive element for motivation, but the main focus is on combining access skills, visual and auditory skills, memory and attention to make the device produce the required message. Gradually the child is given more responsibility for the process. For example, we might initially give specific prompts about when to operate a switch, fading them until the child manages the timing unaided. With vocabulary, the easiest task is to locate a named word or phrase; later, a picture or action could be shown to indicate the target. Finally, we might describe a situation, and ask 'What would you say?'. Here there might be several appropriate responses.

The next stage introduces the child to using the device in 'real life'. It is rare for an individual to use an alternative system spontaneously. We have to find, or set up, situations where there is a strong motivation to communicate, and where the available vocabulary will be powerfully effective. Even so, the child may not recognize the opportunity without help. To begin with, prompts may need to be very specific. For example, if the class has a regular news time on Monday mornings, the child may have a stored message about what s/he did at the weekend. In this case, there will be a situational prompt – s/he will know when the opportunity is going to arise – and a verbal prompt: 'Tell us what you did at the weekend, Sally'.

There are three ways to make prompts gradually less specific. Firstly, by organizing interactions so that the child is unsure *when* a specific communicative opportunity will arise. For example, s/he might be encouraged to wear a badge which says 'Ask me my name!'. Alternatively, the communicative actions of others may be made less predictable: the child might know that there is a question coming, but not know *which* question. Finally, the greatest challenge occurs when the prompt is in the situation rather than something which is said. For example, if s/he has the message 'Don't forget me!', the prompt might be that other people 'accidentally' miss the child out.

When a child first appears in public with a communication device, other people may not know what to expect. The glamour of technology often leads to high expectations; people may not recognize that even the most sophisticated device will only do what the user can make it do. By this time, the child should have reasonable control of the basics, but s/he may have limited vocabulary, and no experience of using a machine to communicate. Without guidance, people may be disappointed and disillusioned when the child cannot perform. If the child experiences this as failure, s/he may reject the system. It is therefore wise to control situations so that listeners know what they can ask, and the child has opportunities to demonstrate what s/he has learned.

The third and final stage sees the child using the communication device on his or her own initiative, in all situations. To succeed at this level demands considerable interpersonal and pragmatic skills. Most people are very finely tuned to the rules and conventions of interaction within their society. Feelings of discomfort or anxiety can arise immediately if even one of these rules is broken by a communication partner. These feelings of discomfort can quickly influence someone to avoid communicating with that person, or can contribute to communication breakdown. When a child is using an electronic communication device a different set of rules and conventions about interaction apply. The child and his or her communication partners need actively to learn these rules and to learn what to say and do in order to communicate comfortably and successfully within the accepted conventions of interaction. Unfortunately, training often overlooks this crucial third stage. It may be difficult for speaking people to identify the additional skills involved in using a machine to communicate. A number of research projects are currently designing training packages to meet this need.

CHAPTER 12
The experience of mobility

Paul Nisbet

Introduction

When the term 'powered wheelchair' is mentioned, it is not usually in the context of education or social interaction. In schools, electric wheelchairs are often regarded as the sole preserve of physio- or occupational therapists; as a last resort for children with severe physical disabilities who have tried and failed to achieve mobility in other ways; as potentially dangerous disruptions to classroom life; as irritatingly heavy lumps of steel and fabric which always seem to have flat batteries and tyres, and leak acid over the school bus. But as tools for accessing the curriculum? No.

If you hold any of these preconceptions, we hope this chapter will change at least some of them. We will begin by reviewing the importance of mobility in early development and the effect of ordinary powered mobility on children's behaviour. Then we will briefly describe the Smart Wheelchair, what it does (without this, the rest of the chapter makes little sense) and the broad curriculum purpose for using it. Then we will focus on how the chairs are used in the classroom, illustrating key points with short stories about Smart Wheelchair pilots who took part in a recent evaluation of the chairs. We will finish by summarising the learning outcomes which were achieved by the children involved in the research.

Educational purpose

Independent mobility provides access to a rich and stimulating set of experiences for a developing child. Consequently, developmental psychologists link early mobility to understanding of space, objects, causality and self (Piaget 1953b; Mahler et al., 1975), spatial cognition and visuo-vestibular integration (Gibson and Spelke, 1983; Campos and

Bertenthal, 1987; Bertenthal and Bai, 1987). Children with multiple impairments who cannot move, cannot speak and have visual difficulties simply do not have access to these developmental experiences. However, we argue that lack of self-produced locomotion not only limits learning: it actually damages a child's ability to learn. Young children who cannot move have fewer opportunities to explore and control their world, leading to developmental delay. Inability then causes frustration, damages confidence and affects the child's motivation to try new activities and experiences, constricting learning still further. The result is a cycle of deprivation which manifests as the 'learned helplessness' seen in many children with multiple impairments.

Recent studies (Paulsson and Christofferson, 1984; Verburg et al., 1986; Butler, 1984; Douglas and Ryan, 1987; Whiting and Peck, 1988) have shown that powered mobility aids can break into this cycle and restore the motivation essential for learning. However, controlling an ordinary wheelchair with a joystick is beyond many of the children with multiple disabilities who are most at risk from the cycle of deprivation. The purpose of the Smart Wheelchair is to provide these children with mobility, and hence access to learning.

The Smart Wheelchair

The Smart Wheelchair (see Figure 12.1) has been designed by the CALL Centre and the Bioengineering Centre, Edinburgh. It consists of a conventional commercially-available electric wheelchair (Newton Product's 'Badger Cub'), with the standard joystick removed and replaced by a 'Smart Controller' (CALL Centre, 1995). The computer inside the Smart Controller allows a child to drive the chair with the sort of switches more often used for computers or communication aids; with joysticks; or with communication aids and laptop computers. Conversely, the chair has communicative abilities: using a speech synthesizer it confirms instructions, reports events and offers choices to the pilot.

To protect the user, the classroom, and the people within it, sensors can be fitted to the Smart Wheelchair. Collision detectors stop the chair when it hits something and take remedial action if necessary (such as backing off and then turning -- the 'Bump and Turn' tool) and a 'line follower' enables the chair to follow tracks taped to the floor. A recent addition are ultrasonic sensors which detect obstacles and slow or stop the chair before it hits them. As well as providing safeguards, the sensing systems are designed to enhance the mobility opportunities with the chair: we call this augmentative mobility because the child's own abilities are augmented by the machine. The chair is not therefore designed as a mobile robot, but as a partner which shares responsibility for movement with the driver. A key concept is that the boundary of control can be shifted between chair and user as circumstances change and the child develops. We will see how this provides learning opportunities later in the chapter.

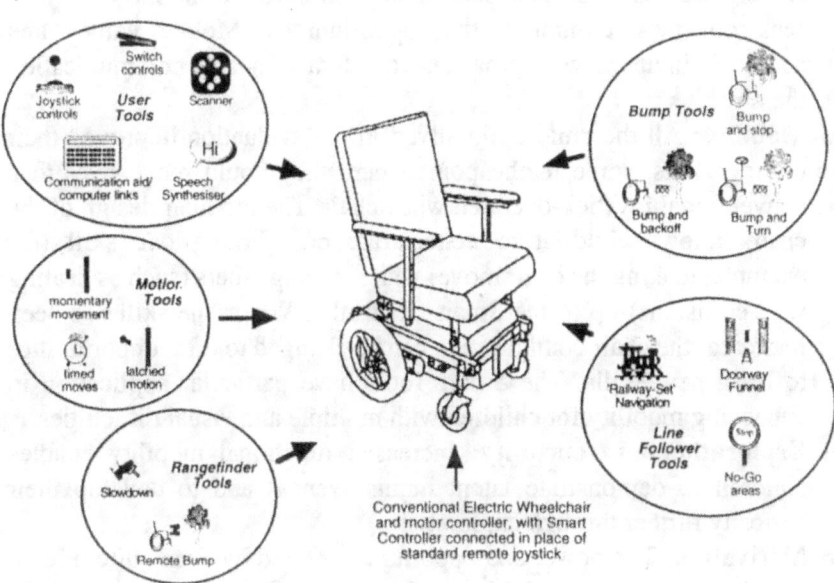

Figure 12.1: Overview of the Smart Wheelchair

Curriculum goals for augmentative mobility

Between 1991 and 1993 the CALL Centre ran a research project evaluating ten Smart Wheelchairs in three Edinburgh special schools. The evaluation was formative, in that it sought to develop chair design, applications and support materials through practical use. The children who used the chairs had different physical, cognitive, communicative and perceptual difficulties and ranged in age from 3.5 to 15 years old. Three children had known or suspected visual problems: we will meet them later. The results (Odor and Watson, 1994a) indicate that augmentative mobility may be used to enhance many aspects of the curriculum, from understanding of cause-and-effect, through peer interaction, to formal problem solving and number work. Fulfilment of these specific curriculum goals relies upon the Smart Wheelchair's capacity to encourage improvements in more general skill areas:

- **Assertiveness:** Mobility is powerful. For the first time perhaps, a child with a Smart Wheelchair can choose to acquiesce to instructions, or assert his or her personality by driving off and ignoring them. More positively, the mobile child can initiate and create new interactions and learning situations.
- **Communication:** As well as promoting assertion and initiation which are themselves important communication skills, a mobile child can seek out new communicative opportunities. Mobile games and activities invite new approaches to interaction and communication therapy.
- **Mobility:** All the children involved in the evaluation improved their driving skills, some to the point where they could move over to a conventional joystick-operated wheelchair. The modular design of the chairs allows children to concentrate on learning one skill (for example, making the chair move) while leaving others (such as dealing with collisions) up to the Smart Controller. When one skill has been mastered, the chair configuration can be changed to offer opportunities to learn new skills. The Smart Tools have particular application in enhancing mobility for children with multiple and visual difficulties.
- **Exploration and curiosity:** Increased functional mobility enables children to demonstrate latent inquisitiveness and to develop their curiosity further through exploration.
- **Motivation:** The power and opportunity offered by even quite limited mobility can motivate children in situations where other stimuli have failed. Such motivation provides the basis on which to build new curriculum goals and experiences.
- **Assessment:** Assessing a multiply disabled child's visual, cognitive and communicative skills can be problematic. A Smart Wheelchair provides unique possibilities for devising activities to test specific skills, such as object recognition and tracking, functionally.

Planning and evaluating learning

We now turn to how general and specific learning goals are determined, methods of tailoring suitable Smart Wheelchair-based activities, and techniques for evaluating outcomes.

All educational interventions aim for constant learning gains and intervention based on augmentative mobility is no different. The process of defining aims, supporting learning and interpreting observations is therefore a cyclical one (see Figure 12.2), anticipating and planning for changes in the child's abilities and skills.

Initial assessment results in a set of curriculum aims from which

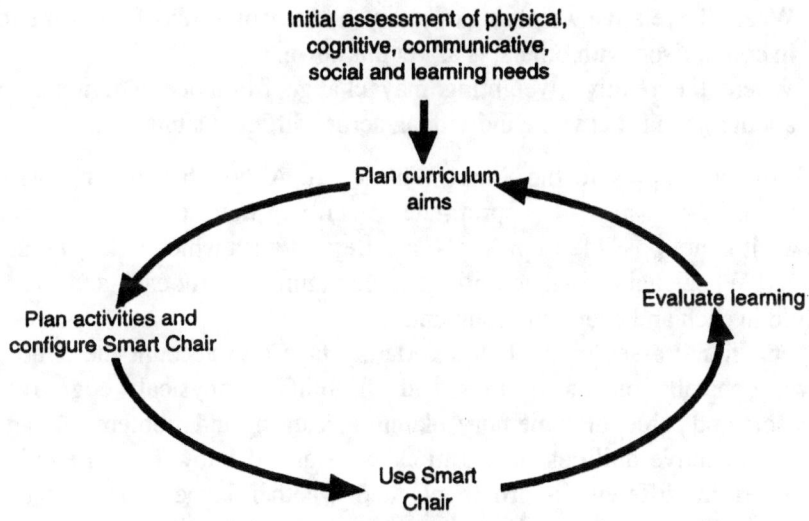

Figure 12.2: The cycle of functional assessment

suitable chair-based activities are devised. The chair's sensors and systems are then configured for these activities, and appropriate seating and switches or controls provided. Use within the classroom may be structured or exploratory, supervised or unsupervised, and in group or individual situations, depending on the curriculum aims. The effect of the intervention is measured functionally within the activities themselves. Consideration of the effects of intervention alters the aims, activities and chair configuration during a session, or causes broader re-assessment of the overall curriculum goals.

Functional assessment

There are many different approaches to assessment and evaluation. For the Smart Wheelchair, we are interested in assessment as a means to an end: in order to gain practical information to help plan subsequent action. We favour a functional approach, considering the child as part of an overall system which includes the chair, the physical environment, and the human resources.

A cycle of functional assessment is most useful in these circumstances:

- When the subject under investigation is relatively new.
- Where few assessment criteria exist.
- Where there is much interaction amongst different areas of assessment.
- Where there are many different areas to be assessed.

- Where the relative weighting to be given to any one area of assessment, in comparison with others, is as yet unknown.
- Where the relative weighting may change from one individual to another, and for any one individual, across different situations.

All of these apply to the Smart Wheelchair. Although it is clear why functional assessment is appropriate, describing how to do it is harder since it is not possible to prescribe a battery of tests which will generate Smart Wheelchair-based activities and configurations for each and every child in each and every environment.

Functional assessment should certainly take into account the child's own constellation of abilities and disabilities: physical; cognitive; sensory and perceptual; memory, planning, learning and problem solving; communicative abilities. In addition, we want to know how the child behaves in different environments and whether some aspect of the context (such as cluttered or clear, familiar or unfamiliar space, or a specific carer or staff member) appears to affect performance. If so, can the positive elements be identified and transferred to other contexts? Lastly, it is important to identify what resources are available since they also have bearing on the successful take-up and use of the technology: these include funding, technical support, time for staff training and opportunities for the child to use the chair within the current time-tabled curriculum.

Recording and analysing the effect of all these factors are problematic because of the sheer quantity of data and the interaction between variables. For the evaluation project, the school staff used diary sheets to record length, location, peers and staff present, activity, and chair configuration for each Smart Wheelchair session. As well as stimulating the process of functional assessment, analysis of the diary sheets enabled the team to relate learning outcomes to environmental variants such as number of chair sessions and time on task.

Curriculum planning

Although we believe that no child is too severely disabled to benefit from using a Smart Wheelchair, some children are likely to gain more than others. The previous section suggested that passive, de-motivated, frustrated children with severe impairments are the most likely candidates. We should not forget use by more able children using the chair for mobility or mobility training. Initial identification, assessment and goal setting involves all members of the child's school team, discussing and sharing aims in order to articulate precise goals for Smart

Wheelchair work. Different schools have different procedures for assessment and planning: during the project, we used developmental profiles to collect information and aims from the staff involved with each child. In a few cases the profiles contained statements drawn from standardized tests (of intelligence or perception, for example) but mostly they were based on staff observations.

Resolving the aims given in the profiles with the staff team generated a summary set of descriptions and aims for each child. By compiling a second profile at the end of the project, we were able to estimate changes that occurred during intervention.

Kenneth was a ten year old quadriplegic boy with overlying right hemiplegia. There were doubts about his vision and visuo-perception. He was one of three children in a 'Mobility Training Group' who had previously tried and failed to master control of a conventional electric wheelchair. The school team hoped the Smart Wheelchair would help develop driving skills.

Graeme was eight years old when referred to the Smart Wheelchair project. He had cerebral palsy with severe motor and learning difficulties. He required a spinal jacket to give him head control; rarely responded to visual stimuli; had few communication skills; and unknown cognition. It was not clear whether his lack of visual activity was due to impairment or lack of interest. The school team hoped that the chair would motivate Graeme and encourage responsiveness and participation, and give opportunities to assess his vision, perception and cognition.

Alan was fifteen and a half years old when referred to the Smart Wheelchair project. He was described as a severe spastic quadriplegic with postural deformities. He was an alert young man interested in people and his surroundings. He communicated using facial expression and vocalization, although he did not have a yes or no response. Little was known about his vision and perception although it was thought he had no problems. Aims for Smart Wheelchair work included developing: Alan's concentration and attention; his use of a switch for scanning access; and his communication, including the use of a suitable voice output aid.

Seating and controls

It is not appropriate within this book to describe assessment for seating in detail since we are focusing on classroom teaching practices. It is clear that a stable, functional seat is essential for good control. The Smart Wheelchair is based upon a commercial chassis for which a range of standard seat sizes and supports are available. The CAPS II adjustable seating system may also be used. Sometimes no commercial solution exists: all of the children in our evaluation required custom-built seating designed by the Bioengineering Centre in Edinburgh.

Assessing for controls is also beyond the scope of this short chapter. Usually, we would begin with a switch which the child has already used successfully for some other purpose, keeping in mind that we want to increase the number of switches to provide greater control.

Kenneth was able to grasp and manipulate a joystick, so he began with a large switched joystick (giving good tactile and proprioceptive feedback), gated forwards only.

Graeme was already using a pneumatic squeeze switch to control a computer and toys and this was transferred to his Smart Wheelchair.

Alan had difficulty targeting and releasing ordinary hit switches. He had used a mercury tilt switch to detect arm raising, but found it difficult to control. His most reliable voluntary movement was flexion and extension of his left index finger so we designed a switch, mounted on a glove, to detect this action.

Maximising mobility and opportunities for learning

We said earlier that mobility is about empowerment and independence. It follows (and our research results bear this out) that more control over mobility gives more independence, which in turn offers better opportunities for learning. Therefore, one aim for most Smart Wheelchair users should be to develop and maximize control over the chair (both directly using controls, and indirectly with strategic use of augmentative tools). There are other reasons for explicitly aiming to develop driving ability: it is a goal with clear worth, it is straightforward to understand and evaluate progress and it requires development of a whole range of skills (see Figure 12.3) which, once learnt using the Smart Wheelchair, can be transferred to other areas of the curriculum. So although independent mobility may not be an end in itself, the means by which it is achieved produces useful learning outcomes.

We might think of this process of skill acquisition as a progression which begins with a user who has little experience of technology or cause-and-effect using it, and ends ideally with a child driving an ordinary powered wheelchair safely and effectively. Figure 12.4 illustrates the skill progression of Kenneth, Graeme and Alan, as user controls and the Smart Wheelchair systems were changed throughout the intervention. The basic pattern, which was repeated across all the children in the evaluation, was a gradual shifting of control from chair to child as the child's mastery and control improved.

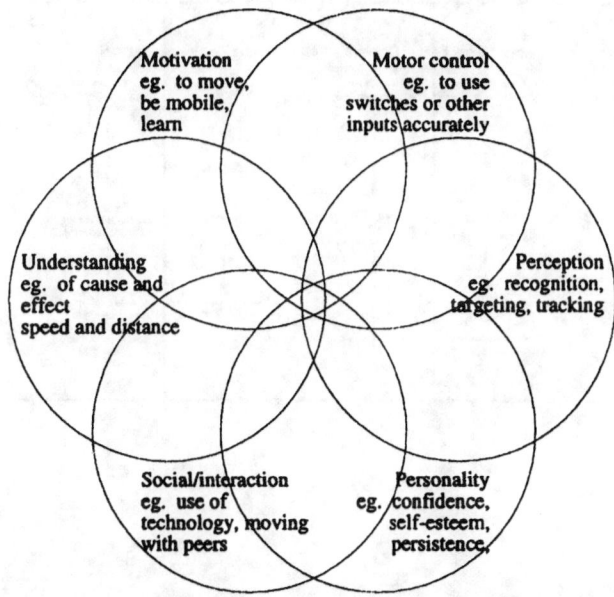

Figure 12.3: Driving skills

Some children start with a single switch and very little control, others begin some way along the progression with several switches. Some reach the end and achieve full control without Smart systems; others plateau. Some, perhaps with a degenerative condition, might start at the 'end' and move towards making greater use of the chair's systems.

To facilitate this sort of progression, the practitioner must understand what the different Smart tools do and how they may be used to achieve specific learning outcomes. We cannot describe the complete range here (*The Wheelchair Playbook*, Odor and Watson, 1994b) and *Guide for Mobility Training*, Odor and Watson, 1994c) give a fuller description) but we will give examples to illustrate the approach taken in the next section.

We believe that this concept of shared control, and of transferring responsibility for control between chair and pilot, is the key to productive use of Smart Wheelchairs. There is no single Smart Wheelchair, but rather a set of controls and systems – 'user tools' and 'chair tools' – which are chosen and combined to suit an individual child and their curriculum aims at that time. Different children require different controls and chair tools, and as the child develops new skills, so the configuration changes to present new learning opportunities.

So although the Smart Wheelchair's systems can be used to give a degree of functional mobility to children with severe disabilities, they are really designed to let children demonstrate latent abilities and develop

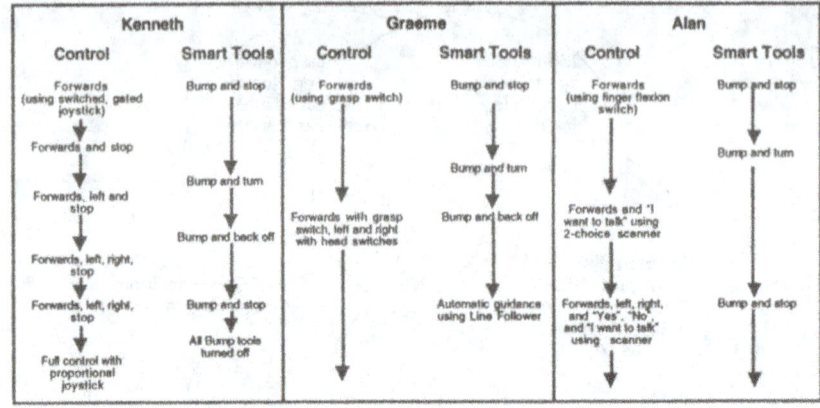

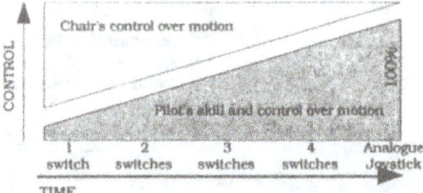

Figure 12.4: Skill progression

new ones. The basic 'Bump and Turn' tool, for example, is of limited use as an aid to functional mobility since it always backs off and turns the chair through the same angle, but it can provide a powerful method for single switch users to explore their environment, or as an introduction to steering. Similarly, while the line follower can be used by a child, operating a single switch, to move around the school, we hope that the experience of doing so will help develop switch use, self-confidence (through unsupervised, independent mobility along the track) and an understanding of the personal value of achieving independent mobility.

Task design and chair configuration

Choosing appropriate controls and chair-based tools is vital. We will illustrate this process by looking at how the initial sessions were planned for the three children we met earlier.

For most Smart Wheelchair users, the first few sessions will be designed to introduce the experience of mobility gently, to build confidence. To a small child who has never been mobile, particularly one with visual difficulties, driving an electric wheelchair may feel something like your first time driving a car (assuming the reader is a driver): perhaps excitement tempered by fear, anxiety and disbelief that you will ever manage to co-ordinate the controls while simultaneously avoiding hitting other vehicles, looking for road signs and markings, and planning your route. In your first lesson it is likely the instructor operated the pedals while you steered, to help you learn one thing at a time. So it is with the Smart Wheelchair: the first sessions should allow the child to concentrate on something basic, like making the chair move (using the Timed tool perhaps), without having to worry about finer points of control like stopping, steering or planning what to do with the mobility. These come later.

Kenneth had already tried controlling a powered chair, so he started with the 'momentary' tool giving him control over both moving and stopping, and 'bump and turn' managing collisions and introducing new directions.

Graeme's passivity suggested that it was vital to achieve successful, fun experiences over which he had control, in order to motivate him and build confidence. He began by watching his helper drive the chair, but showed little or no interest (possibly due to visual impairment). The diary reports that his facial and eye expression changed immediately he sat on his helper's lap and experienced movement of the chair. He responded to her commentary with a fairly consistent 'yes' and 'no'. After a few sessions, he sat in the chair himself and used his squeeze switch with 'timed' control, leaving stopping to the chair. He was responsive and smiling and needed little encouragement to operate his switch. These small steps were regarded as major successes since for the first time he had shown evidence of intrinsic motivation to tackle an activity over which he had complete control.

Alan was introduced to the chair slowly, first by watching his helper drive it using 'Timed Motion', then sitting on her lap driving it himself, then driving solo. Although his mobility was limited to going forward only, he explored it fully, driving and stopping to look for some time at everyday objects.

Structuring and supporting learning

As these stories show, it is important to take account of children's motivations and personalities when planning and running Smart Wheelchair sessions and to choose appropriate chair tools, activities and styles of interaction. Some issues and examples are given below.

Directive and nondirective approaches

We would hope that most children are motivated intrinsically by the mobility itself and therefore need little direction or encouragement from staff. (It may be argued that children need to be taught how to use the controls, but we suggest that curiosity is better stimulated if the child can explore them without interruption or distraction).

In his first session driving solo, Alan demonstrated previously unknown assertiveness by refusing to move until staff moved away from his chair. His ability to explore all the aspects of a new tool and develop strategies for dealing with problems and limitations was to be repeated many times throughout the project.

In one school, the speech and language therapists routinely use chairs during nondirective therapy sessions, taking the lead for the session activities from the child's movement.

Interactive games

Setting up and playing mobility games serves several purposes. First, games encourage social interaction. Second, games can make early mobility where the child has only limited control over the chair more interesting and challenging (although some children still prefer freedom to structure).

After a few weeks practising with his single switch Alan started using 'Bump and Turn' as an introduction to steering. The school staff set up a game of skittles, arranged so that when he knocked one over, the chair would back off and turn to face the next one. Alan quickly showed that he understood how to use the tool, but was not overly thrilled with the activity. He was more motivated on a later 'free' session where he managed to bump and turn round a complete circuit of the school.

Thirdly, games can allow the practitioner to structure the session in order to assess specific skills in functional, motivating contexts. The Speech and Language therapist wanted to assess Nigel's vision, so she started playing hide and seek. As he drove down the corridor, he shouted out that he could see her hand sticking out from the classroom door.

Lastly, games are fun for the child. Cameron laughed and giggled as he used his single switch and 'Bump and Back Off' to run into the researcher again and again.

The Smart Wheelchair Playbook and *Guide for Mobility Training* contain ideas for activities and adapted games.

Opportunities for cooperation and communication

The chair – child combination is viewed as a partnership, sharing control over mobility. The child instructs the chair using the switch and the chair responds by moving, and reporting via the speech synthesizer 'Observer' (e.g. 'Oops, I've hit something, I'll back off and try turning right'). Although limited and artificial, such interaction does develop early turn-taking and attention skills.

After one occasion when the batteries were flat on the synthesizer Alan's mother reported that he seemed lost without 'his' voice.

The practitioner can also partner the child when tackling tasks. Jack's practitioner introduced steering by negotiating with him which way he wanted to turn, and then pressing a switch to rotate the chair until he indicated to stop.

Mobility gives a child something to talk about, and different people to talk with. Since Alan used his finger to both drive the chair, and initiate communication, he could not say 'hello' to someone without simultaneously driving away from them. To get around this we built a two-choice scanner on a Macintosh Powerbook, giving 'move' and an attention-grabbing bleep. The choices were presented with digitized pictures and speech because little was known about Alan's visual perception. Subsequently, the scanner was extended to give him control over forwards, left and right, and three digitized messages: 'I want to talk', 'yes' and 'no'.

Structure, supervision and free use

In the early stages when control is limited, structured, supervised sessions can help to reassure the child (and staff) and build confidence. Unsupervised driving is important as the child develops, to give experience in moving independently.

As Kenneth's skills developed, control over turning left, then right, then reversing was introduced. Staff noticed that he used 'shore-lining' when driving around the school and he then began to use the chair freely within the classroom, outside the structured driving lessons. We hypothesize that his previous failure with a powered chair was due not only to motor difficulties, but also lack of confidence caused by his visual impairment. (He drove well in cluttered, familiar environments but appeared 'lost' in large, bare unknown locations without familiar landmarks. Bright light also affected his accuracy.) Structuring of the early chair sessions (through limiting his control and environment and giving instruction) enabled him to develop control over the joystick, but more importantly, confidence in the chair and his ability to drive it. After three months practice, Kenneth no longer needed the Smart systems, so they were replaced with an ordinary analogue joystick, which he controlled with aplomb. The ultimate aim of the intervention had been achieved, and Kenneth was referred for a conventional electric wheelchair.

However, it is not necessary for the child to have a high level of control to experience unsupervised independent functional mobility: the line follower can provide it to a certain extent.

Graeme had started to use head switches for steering but the staff felt his control was not accurate enough (possibly due to perceptual problems) and that he was becoming frustrated. It was suggested that a Line Follower would give more independent mobility around the school while allowing him to leave the line at any point and drive independently with his head switches. The diary suggests that he enjoyed the relative security and relaxation of being able to drive safely along the school corridor without having to continually adjust direction.

Evaluating learning

We discussed evaluation earlier, and suggested that it should take place naturally as part of the intervention process. We described some of the evaluation techniques used in the research project to review progress and plan the next stages of the work: written diaries, videos, team reviews and standardized driving tests.

To finish, we present a summary of the learning outcomes for each of the ten children involved in the main evaluation (see Figure 12.5). The charts are made by comparing profiles pre- and post- intervention, set against the main environmental influences, which are disruption and time-on-task. Although the wide spread of time-on-task reflects different lengths of intervention period for each child and maybe inconsistent diary keeping, there is no doubt that children who had access to their chairs learned more. (David's total time-on-task is so large because he achieved

Name		David	Alan	Graeme	Sara	Jack	Stephen	William	Cameron	Adam	Ross
Total time on task (hours)		1087	172	83	75	37	34	26	20	19.5	11
	lack of continuity					√	√	√	√	√	√
	illness				√			√		√	√
	staff/class changes	√	√	√	√			√	√		√
Mobility skills											
	Three point turn	•									
	Reverse	•									
	Twin curve/multiple turns	•	Δ	ø	ø	Δ					
	Sharp left/right turn	•	•	Δ	ø	•					
	Pointing	•	•	Δ	•	•	Δ	ø	ø	Δ	ø
	Straight line moves	•	•	•	•	•	•	ø	•	•	ø
	Control over stops	•	•	•	•	•	•	•	•	•	Δ
	Simple moves	•	•	•	•	•	•	•	•	•	•
Key:	• = skill consistently demonstrated Δ = current therapy, improving ø = current therapy, mixed results										
General developmental skills											
	Assertiveness / motivation	good	good	fair	fair	fair	fair	mixed	mixed	fair	none
	Concentration / attention	good	good	fair	fair	mixed	mixed	fair	mixed	fair	
	Communication	good	fair	slight	slight	fair	fair	fair	fair	slight	slight
	Socialisation	good	good	?	mixed	?	mixed	fair	none	slight	
	Physical skills	good	slight	fair	mixed	fair	fair	slight	slight	mixed	

Key	
good	consistent improvements against this child's baseline
fair	improvements recorded - occasionally spasmodic
slight	some improvements, slow progress
mixed	improvements localised / poor transfer to other contexts / inconsistent progress or regressions
none	no improvements
regressed	child now consistently worse against baseline
?	< no reports

Figure 12.5: Learning outcomes

full control using an analogue joystick and used his chair all day at school and home, whereas the other children's access was more restricted by other curricular activities.)

Since the range of children and environments is so wide it is not possible to attribute changes directly to the Smart Wheelchair (apart from mobility, since none of the children used a mobility aid prior to intervention). Nevertheless, we are in no doubt that augmentative mobility can provide significant developmental improvements for severely disabled children.

It is clear that practice is essential if a child is to develop his or her full potential with the chair. To achieve this in a school, management and staff must be convinced that augmentative mobility can help fulfil existing curriculum goals, as well as create new ones which were previously thought impractical or impossible. We hope that this chapter has given a flavour of how such integration is approached: more detailed discussion is available in the CALL Smart Wheelchair publications, and in particular, in *Moving Smartly through 5-14* (Odor et al., 1995).

References

Ainsworth, M.D.S. (1982) 'Attachment: Retrospect and prospect'. In: C.M.Parkes and J.Stevenson-Hinde (eds.) *The Place of Attachment in Human Behavior.* New York: Basic Books.

Aitken, S. (1995) 'Educational assessment of deafblind learners'. In: D. Etheridge (ed.) *The Education of Dual Sensory Impaired Children: Recognising and Developing Ability.* London: David Fulton.

Aitken, S. and McDevitt, A. (1995) *Using IT to Support Visually Impaired Learners: Books 1, 2, and 3.* Birmingham: University of Birmingham.

Anokhin, P.K. (1969) 'Cybernetics and the integrative activity of the brain'. In: M.Cole and I.Maltzman (eds.) *Contemporary Soviet Psychology.* New York: Basic Books.

Astington, J. (1994) *The Child's Discovery of the Mind.* London: Fontana Press.

Baumgart, D., Johnson, J. and Helmstetter, E. (1990) *Augmentative and Alternative Communication Systems for Persons with Moderate and Severe Disabilities.* Baltimore: Paul Brookes Publishing Company.

Bertenthal, B.J. and Bai, D.L. (1987) 'Visual-vestibular integration in early development'. *Proceedings of RESNA First Northwest Regional Conference: Childhood Powered Mobility, Developmental, Technical and Clinical Perspectives.* 43-61. Seattle: RESNA.

Beukelman, D.R. and Mirenda, P. (1992) *Augmentative and Alternative Communication.* Baltimore: Paul Brookes Publishing Company.

Blenkhorn, P. (1986) 'The RCEVH project on micro-computer systems and computer assisted learning', *British Journal of Visual Impairment,* **4**(3), 101-103.

Bozic, N. (1993) 'Expressive communications', *Special Children,* **69**, 30-33.

Bozic, N. (1995) 'Using microcomputers in naturalistic language intervention: The trialling of a new approach', *British Journal of Learning Disabilities,* **23**(2), 59-62.

Bozic, N. and McCall, S. (1993) 'Microcomputer software: developing braille reading skills', *British Journal of Special Education,* **20**(2), 58.

Bozic, N., Hill, E.W., and Tobin, M.J., (1993) 'Pre-school visually impaired children: Visual stimulation and micro-computers', *Child: Care, Health and Development,* **19**(1), 25-35.

Bozic, N., Cooper, L., Etheridge, A. and Selby, A. (1995) 'Microcomputer-based joint activities in communication intervention with visually impaired children: a case study', *Child Language Teaching and Therapy,* **11**(1), 91-105.

Bremner, J.G. (1988) *Infancy.* Oxford: Blackwell.

Brinker, R.P. and Lewis, M. (1982) 'Making the world work with microcomputers: A learning prothesis for handicapped infants', *Exceptional Children,* **49**(2), 163-170.

Brown, A.L. and Ferrara, R.A. (1985) 'Diagnosing zones of proximal development'. In: J.V. Wertsch (ed.) *Culture, Cognition and Communication.* Cambridge: Cambridge University Press.

Bruner, J.S. (1966) 'On cognitive growth'. In: J.S. Bruner, R.R. Oliver and P.M. Greenfield (eds.) *Studies in Cognitive Growth.* New York: John Wiley & Sons.

Bruner, J.S. (1975) 'The ontogenesis of speech acts', *Journal of Child Language,* **2**, 1-19.

Bruner, J.S. (1978) 'From communication to language: a psychological perspective'. In: I.Markova (ed.) *The Social Context of Language.* New York: Wiley.

Bruner, J.S. (1983) *Child's Talk: Learning to Use Language.* Oxford: Oxford University Press.

Bruner, J.S. (1984) 'Vygotsky's Zone of Proximal Development: the hidden agenda'. In:

B. Rogoff and J. Wertsch (eds.) *Children's Learning in the 'Zone of Proximal Development'*. San Francisco: Jossey-Bass Inc.

Butler, C. (1984) 'Effects of powered mobility on self-initiated behaviours of very young children with locomotor disability'. *Developmental Medicine and Child Neurology*, **28**, 325-332.

CALL Centre (1995) *Smart Wheelchair User Handbook*. University of Edinburgh: CALL Centre.

Campos, J.J. and Bertenthal, B.J. (1987) 'Locomotion and psychological development in infancy'. *Proceedings of RESNA First Northwest Regional Conference: Childhood Powered Mobility, Developmental, Technical and Clinical Perspectives*. 11-42. Seattle: RESNA.

Cole, M. and Griffin, P. (1980) 'Cultural amplifiers reconsidered'. In: D.R.Olson (ed.) *The Social Foundations of Language and Thought*. New York: Norton.

Cole, M. and Griffin, P. (1984) 'Current activity for the future: The zo-ped'. In: B. Rogoff and J.V. Wertsch (eds.) *Children's Learning in the 'Zone of Proximal Development'*. San Francisco: Jossey-Bass Inc.

Coupe, J., Barton, L., Barber, M., Collins, L., Levy, D., and Murphy, D. (1985) *The Affective Communication Assessment*. Manchester: Manchester Education Committee.

Coupe, J., Barton, L. and Walker, S. (1988) 'Teaching first meanings'. In: J. Coupe and J. Goldbart (eds.) *Communication Before Speech*. London: Chapman and Hall.

Crook, C. (1994) *Computers and the Collaborative Experience of Learning: A Psychological Perspective*. London: Routledge.

Cunningham, C.C. and Glenn, S.M. (1985) 'Parent involvement and early intervention'. In: D. Lane and B. Stratford (eds.) *Current Approaches to Down's Syndrome*. Eastbourne: Holt, Rinehart, Winston.

Cunningham, C.C., Hutchinson, R. and Kewin, J. (1991) 'Recreation for people with profound and severe learning difficulties: the Whittington Hall Snoezelen project'. In: R.Hutchinson (ed.) *The Whittington Hall Snoezelen Project: A Report from Inception to the End of the First Twelve Months*. Chesterfield: North Derbyshire Health Authority.

Daniels, H. (in press) 'Psychology for social purposes'. In: H. Daniels (ed.) *An Introduction to Vygotsky*. London: Routledge.

Davydov, V.V. (1988) 'Problems of developmental teaching: The experience of theoretical and experimental psychological research', *Soviet Education*, Vol.XXX, **(8)**, 3-87; **(9)**, 3-56; **(10)**, 2-42.

DeCasper, A.J. and Carstens, A.A. (1981) 'Contingencies of stimulation: Effects on learning and emotion in neonates', *Infant Behavior and Development*, **4**, 19-35.

Detheridge, T. (1995) 'Keeping track and moving on'. In: *Extending Horizons*. Litton, Derbyshire: Imagination Technology Publications.

Detheridge, T. and Hopkins, C., (1991) 'Switch control'. In: T. Detheridge (ed.) *Technology in support of the National Curriculum for Students with Severe Learning Difficulties*. Coventry: NCET.

Dewart, H. and Summers, S. (1988) *The Pragmatics Profile of Early Communication Skills*. Windsor: NFER-Nelson.

Dickens, J. (1995) *Using a computer with multi-disabled visually impaired pupils*. Unpublished B.Phil.(Ed.) Dissertation, School of Education, University of Birmingham.

Dickens, J. (1993) 'Using centre soundbook', *RCEVH Centre Software Newsletter*, **32**, 4, School of Education, University of Birmingham (mimeo).

Douglas, G. and Greaney, J. (1995) 'Computer-aided braille reading', *Paper presented at the 9th European Conference on Reading*. Budapest, July 24-26, 1995.

Douglas, J. and Ryan, M. (1987) 'A pre-school severely disabled boy and his powered wheelchair: A case study', *Child: Care, Health and Development*, **13**(5), 303-309.

Elstner, W. (1983) 'Abnormalities in the verbal communication of visually impaired children'. In: Mills, A. (ed.) *Language Acquisition in the Blind Child: Normal and Deficient*. London: Croom Helm.

Engestrom, J. (1991) 'Non scolae sed vitae discimus: Toward overcoming the encapsulation of school learning', *Learning and Instruction*, **1**, 243-259.

Erin, J.N. (1986) 'Frequencies and types of questions in the language of visually impaired children', *Journal of Visual Impairment and Blindness*, **80**, 670-674.

Evans, P. (1993) 'Some implications of Vygotsky's work for special education'. In: H.Daniels (ed.) *Charting the Agenda: Educational Activity after Vygotsky*. London: Routledge.

Evans. P. and Ware, J. (1987) *Special Care Provision – The Education of Children with Profound and Multiple Learning Difficulties*. Windsor: NFER.

Gibson, E. and Spelke, E. (1983) 'The development of perception'. In: J. Flavell and E. Markman (eds.) *Handbook of Child Psychology, Vol. 3, Cognitive Development*. New York: John Wiley.

Glenn, S.M. (1987) 'Activities to encourage children's development within the early sensori-motor period'. In: B.Smith (ed.) *Interactive Approaches to the Education of Children with Severe Learning Difficulties*. Birmingham: Westhill College.

Glenn, S.M. and Cunningham, C.C. (1984a) 'Selective auditory preferences and the use of automated equipment by severely, profoundly and multiply handicapped children'. *Journal of Mental Deficiency Research*, **28**, 281-296.

Glenn, S.M. and Cunningham, C.C. (1984b) 'Special care – but active learning'. *Special Education: Forward Trends*, **11**, 33-36.

Glenn, S.M. and O'Brien, Y. (1994) 'Microcomputers: do they have a part to play in the education of children with PMLDs?' In: J.Ware (ed.) *Educating Children with Profound and Multiple Learning Difficulties*. London: David Fulton.

Goldbart, J. (1988a) 'Communication for a purpose'. In: J. Coupe and J. Goldbart (eds.) *Communication Before Speech*. London: Chapman and Hall.

Goldbart, J. (1988b) 'Re-examining the development of early communication'. In: J. Coupe and J. Goldbart (eds.) *Communication Before Speech*, London: Chapman and Hall.

Goldbart, J. (1994) 'Opening the communication curriculum to students with PMLDs'. In: J. Ware (ed.) *Educating Children with Profound and Multiple Learning Difficulties*. London: David Fulton.

Haggar, L.E. and Hutchinson, R.B. (1991) 'Snoezelen: an approach to the provision of a leisure resource for people with profound and multiple handicaps', *Mental Handicap*, **19**, 51-55.

Halle, J.W. (1984) 'Arranging the natural environment to occasion language: giving severely language-delayed children reasons to communicate', *Seminars in Speech and Language*, **5**, 185-196.

Halliday, M.A.K. (1975) *Learning How to Mean: Explorations in the Development of Language*. London: Edward Arnold.

Harris, J. (1990) *Early Language Development: Implications for Educational and Clinical Practice*. London: Routledge.

Hubel, D.H. and Wiesel, T.N. (1963) 'Receptive fields of cells in striate cortex of very young, visually inexperienced kittens', *Journal of Neurophysiology*, **6**, 1003-1017.

Hulsegge, J. and Verheul, A. (1987) *Snoezelen: Another World.* Chesterfield: Rompa UK Publications.

Hutchinson, R. and Haggar, L. (1994) 'The development and evaluation of a Snoezelen leisure resource for people with severe multiple disability.' In: R. Hutchinson and J. Kewin (eds.) *Sensations and Disability.* Chesterfield: Rompa UK publications.

Hutchinson, R. and Kewin, J. (eds.) (1994) *Sensations and Disability.* Chesterfield: Rompa UK publications.

Kaye, K. (1982) *The Mental and Social Life of Babies: How Parents Create Persons.* London: Methuen and Co.

Kewin, J. (1994) 'Snoezelen – The reason and method'. In: R. Hutchinson and J. Kewin (eds.) *Sensations and Disability.* Chesterfield: Rompa UK Publications.

Kiernan, C. (1988) 'Assessment for teaching communication skills'. In: J. Coupe and J. Goldbart (eds.) *Communication Before Speech.* London: Chapman and Hall.

Kiernan, C. and Jones, M.C. (1982) *The Behaviour Assessment Battery (Revised Edition).* Windsor: NFER-Nelson.

Kiernan, C. and Reid, B. (1987a) *The Pre-verbal Communication Schedule (PVCS).* Windsor: NFER-Nelson.

Kiernan, C. and Reid, B. (1987b) *The Pre-verbal Communication Schedule (PVCS) Manual.* Windsor: NFER-Nelson.

Kiernan, C., Reid, B. and Goldbart, J. (1987) *Foundations of Language and Communication.* Manchester: BIMH/Manchester University Press.

Kim, Y.T. and Lombardino, L.J. (1991) 'The efficacy of script contexts in language comprehension intervention with children who have mental retardation', *Journal of Speech and Hearing Research*, **34**, 845-857.

Knox, J.E. and Stevens, C. (1993) 'Vygotsky and Soviet Russian defectology: An introduction'. In: L.S.Vygotsky, *The Collected Works of L S Vygotsky. Volume 2: The Fundamentals of Defectology (Abnormal Psychology and Learning Disabilities).* London: Plenum Press.

Kozulin, A. (1986) 'The concept of activity in Soviet psychology: Vygotsky, his disciples and critics', *American Psychologist*, **41**(3), 264-274.

Kozulin, A. (1990) *Vygotsky's Psychology: A Biography of Ideas.* London: Harvester.

Lave, J. and Wenger, E.(1991) *Situated Learning: Legitimate Peripheral Participation.* Cambridge: Cambridge University Press

Leont'ev, A.N. (1981a) *Problems of the Development of Mind.* Moscow: Progress Publishers.

Leont'ev, A.N. (1981b) 'The problem of activity in psychology'. In: J.V.Wertsch (ed.) *The Concept of Activity in Soviet Psychology.* Armonk, New York: M.E.Sharpe Inc.

Lubovsky, I. (1993) Interview conducted at the Institute of Defectology, Moscow.

Lunt, I. (1993) 'The practice of assessment'. In: H. Daniels (ed.) *Charting the Agenda: Educational Activity after Vygotsky.* London: Routledge.

Luria, A.R. (1977) *Cognitive Development: Its Cultural and Social Foundations.* Cambridge, MA: Harvard University Press.

Luria, A.R. (1979) *The Making of Mind.* Cambridge, MA: Harvard University Press.

Luria, A.R. and Yudovich, F. (1971) *Speech and the Development of Mental Progression in the Child.* Harmondsworth: Penguin.

Mahler, M., Pine, F., Bergman, A. (1975) *The Psychological Birth of the Human Infant.* New York: Basic Books.

McCall, S., McLinden, M. and Stone, J. (1994) *Moon as a Route to Literacy Project. Final Report to Leverhulme Trust.* Unpublished Report, School of Education,

University of Birmingham.
McCall, S., McLinden, M. and Stone, J. (1995) *The Moon Cats Teaching Pack.* London: RNIB.
McClenny, C.S., Roberts, J.E. and Layton, T.L. (1992) 'Unexpected events and their effect on children's language', *Child Language Teaching and Therapy,* **8**(3), 229-245.
Mills, A. (1988) 'Visual handicap'. In: D. Bishop and K. Mogford (eds.) *Language Development in Exceptional Circumstances.* Hove: LEA.
Newman, D., Griffin, P., and Cole, M. (1989) *The Construction Zone : Working for Change in School.* Cambridge: Cambridge University Press.
Newson, E. (1993) 'Play-based assessment in the special needs classroom'. In: J. Harris (ed.) *Innovations in Educating Children with Severe Learning Difficulties.* Chorley: Lisieux Hall.
Newson, J. (1978) 'Dialogue and development'. In: A. Locke (ed.) *Action, Gesture and Symbol: the Emergence of Language.* New York: Academic Press.
O'Brien, Y., Glenn, S.M. and Cunningham, C.C. (1994) 'Contingency awareness in infants and children with severe and profound learning disabilities'. *International Journal of Disability, Development and Education,* **41**, 231-243.
Odor, J.P. and Watson, M. (1994a) *Learning through Smart Wheelchairs.* University of Edinburgh: CALL Centre.
Odor, J.P. and Watson, M. (1994b) *Learning through Smart Wheelchairs Annex 5: Guides for Mobility Training and Assessment.* University of Edinburgh: CALL Centre.
Odor, J.P. and Watson, M. (1994c) *Learning through Smart Wheelchairs Annex 6: The Wheelchair Playbooks.* University of Edinburgh: CALL Centre.
Odor, J.P., Kristoffersen, K., Pinkerton, S. and Hand, A. (1995) *Moving Smartly Through 5-14.* University of Edinburgh: CALL Centre.
Painter, C. (1984) 'Visual assessment with the less able visually handicapped', *RCEVH Centre Software Newsletter* **8**, 7-9, School of Education, University of Birmingham (mimeo).
Pascual-Leone, A. and Torres, F. (1993) 'Plasticity of the sensori-motor cortex representation of the reading finger in braille readers', *Brain,* **16**, 39-52.
Paulsson, K. and Christoffersen, M. (1984) 'Psychosocial aspects of technical aids: how does independent mobility affect the psychosocial and intellectual development of children with physical disabilities?', *Proceedings of the 2nd International Conference of RESNA.* 282-285. Seattle: RESNA.
Piaget, J. (1953a) 'How children form mathematical concepts', *Scientific American,* **189**(5), 74-79, (November, 1953).
Piaget, J. (1953b) *The Origin of Intelligence in the Child.* London: Routledge and Kegan Paul Ltd.
Research Centre for the Education of the Visually Handicapped (1993, 1994) *Centre SoundBook Manual.* University of Birmingham: School of Education.
Rogow, S. (1980) 'Language development in blind multihandicapped children: A model of co-active intervention', *Child: Care, Health and Development,* **6**(5), 301-308.
Seligman, M. (1975) *Helplessness: On Depression, Development and Death.* San Francisco: Freeman.
Shepherd, P.A. and Fagan, J.F. (1981) 'Visual pattern detection and recognition memory in children with profound mental retardation', *International Review of Research in Mental Retardation,* **10**, 31-60.
Smith, C. (1993) *Multi Sensory Environments,* Unpublished Paper, Coventry: National Council for Educational Technology.

Snow, C.E. (1989) 'Understanding social interaction and language acquisition; sentences are not enough'. In: M.E. Bornstein and J.S. Bruner (eds.) *Interaction in Human Development.* Hove: Lawrence Erlbaum.

Snyder-McLean, L.K., Solomonson, B., McLean, J.E. and Sack, S. (1984) 'Structuring joint action routines: A strategy for facilitating communication and language development in the classroom', *Seminars in Speech and Language,* **5**, 213-228.

Spencer, S. and Ross, M. (1989). 'Assessing functional vision using micro-computers', *British Journal of Special Education,* **16**(2), 68-70.

Tudge, J.R.H. (1992) 'Processes and consequences of peer collaboration: A Vygotskian analysis', *Child Development,* **63**, 1364-1379.

Tudge, J.R.H. and Winterhoff, P.A. (1993) 'Vygotsky, Piaget, and Bandura: perspectives on the relations between the social world and cognitive development', *Human Development,* **36**(2), 61-81.

Urwin, C. (1983) 'Dialogue and cognitive functioning in the early language development of three blind children'. In A.E. Mills (ed.) *Language Acquisition in the Blind Child.* Beckenham: Croom Helm.

Uzgiris, I.C. and Hunt, J.McV. (1975) *Assessment in Infancy: Ordinal Scales of Psychological Development.* Urbana, IL: University of Illinois Press.

Van der Veer, R. and Van Ijzendoorn, M.H. (1985) 'Vygotsky's theory of the higher psychological processes: Some criticisms', *Human Development,* **28**, 1-9.

Van Dijk, J. (1965) 'The first steps of deaf-blind children towards language'. *Proceedings of Conference on the Deaf-Blind: Refsnaesskolen, Denmark.* Boston, USA: Perkins School for the Blind.

Verburg, G., Snell, E., Pilkington, M., Milner, M. (1986) 'Effects of powered mobility on young handicapped children and their families.' In: E. Trefler, K. Kozole and E. Snell (eds.) *Selected Readings on Powered Mobility for Children and Adults with Severe Physical Disabilities.* Seattle: RESNA.

Vygotsky, L.S. (1978) *Mind in Society: The Development of Higher Psychological Processes.* Cambridge: Harvard University Press.

Vygotsky, L.S. (1981) 'The genesis of higher mental functions'. In: J.V.Wertsch (ed.) *The Concept of Activity in Soviet Psychology.* Armonk, NY: M.E. Sharpe.

Vygotsky, L.S. (1987) *The Collected Works of L.S. Vygotsky. Volume 1: Problems of General Psychology,* (R.W. Rieber and A.S. Carton, (eds.); N. Minick, (trans.). London: Plenum Press.

Vygotsky, L.S. (1993) *The Collected Works of L.S. Vygotsky. Volume 2: Problems of abnormal psychology and learning disabilities.* (R.W. Rieber & A.S. Carton (eds.); J. Knox and C.B. Stevens (trans.)). London: Plenum Press.

Walker, E.C., Tobin, M.J. and McKennell, A.C. (1992) *Blind and Partially Sighted Children in Britain: The RNIB Survey, Volume 2.* London: HMSO.

Ware, J. (1994) 'Implementing the 1988 Act with pupils with PMLDs'. In: J.Ware (ed.) *Educating Children with Profound and Multiple Learning Difficulties.* London: David Fulton.

Watson, J.S. (1972) 'Smiling, cooing and the game'. *Merrill-Palmer Quarterly,* **18**, 323-329.

Wertsch, J.V. (1985) 'The concept of internalization in Vygotsky's account of the genesis of higher mental functions'. In: J.V.Wertsch (ed.) *Culture, Cognition and Communication.* Cambridge: Cambridge University Press.

Wertsch, J.V. (1995) 'Sociocultural research in the copyright age', *Culture and Psychology,* **1**(1), 81-102.

Whiting, R. and Peck, P. (1988) *The Electric Wheelchair as a Mobility Aid to the Visually Impaired/Multi Disabled Student.* Australia: St. Paul's School for the Blind and Visually Impaired.

Wood, D.J. (1980) 'Social interaction, language, and thought'. In: D.R.Olson (ed.) *The Social Foundations of Language and Thought – Essays in Honor of Jerome S. Bruner.* London: W.W. Norton and Company.

Wood, D. (1988) *How Children Think and Learn.* Oxford: Blackwell.

Wood, D. (1989) 'Social interaction as tutoring'. In: M.H.Bornstein and J.S.Bruner (eds.) *Interaction in Human Development.* Hove: Lawrence Erlbaum.

Wood, D.J., Bruner, J.S. and Ross, G. (1976) 'The role of tutoring in problem solving', *Journal of Child Psychology and Psychiatry,* **17**(2), 89-100.

Wood, D.J., Wood, H.A. and Middleton, D.J. (1978) 'An experimental evaluation of four face-to-face teaching strategies', *International Journal of Behavioural Development,* **1**(2), 131-147.

Yaroshevsky, M. (1989) *Lev Vygotsky.* Moscow: Progress Publishers.

Author Index

Ainsworth, M.D.S. 69
Aitken, S. 63, 118
Anokhin, P.K. 2
Astington, J. 16, 19

Bai, D.L. 144
Baumgart, D. 118
Bertenthal, B.J. 144
Beukelman, D.R. 119–20, 123
Blenkhorn, P. 43
Bozic, N. 14, 19, 44, 63
Bremner, J.G. 69
Brinker, R.P. 70
Brown, A.L. 6
Bruner, J.S. ix, 7, 13–14
Butler, C. 144

CALL Centre 144
Campos, J.J. 143
Carstens, A.A. 70
Cole, M. 7, 9
Coupe, J. 14, 30
Cristoffersen, M. 144
Crook, C. 2, 7
Cunningham, C.C. 70, 72

Daniels, H. xi
Davydov, V.V. xii
DeCasper, A.J. 70
Detheridge, T. 31, 35
Dewart, H. 16–17
Dickens, J. 53–4
Douglas, G. 44
Douglas, J. 144

Elstner, W. 118
Engstrom, J. x
Erin, J.N. 118
Evans, P. 11, 68, 71

Fagan, J.F. 70
Ferrara, R.A. 6

Gibson, E. 143
Glenn, S.M. 28, 70–2
Goldbart, J. 14, 16, 26, 68
Greaney, J. 44
Griffin, P. 7, 9

Haggar, L.E. 72
Halle, J.W. 14
Halliday, M.A.K. 15–16
Harris, J. 15
Hopkins, C. 31
Hubel, D.H. 58
Hulsegge, J. 71–2, 83
Hunt, J.M. 73
Hutchinson, R. 67, 72

Jones, M.C. 30

Kaye, K. 69
Kewin, J. 67, 71–2
Kiernan, C. 15–17, 19, 30, 90
Kim, Y.T. 14
Knox, J.E. xi, xiii
Kozulin, A. ix–x, xii

Lave, J. xii
Leont'ev, A.N. viii, 9

Lewis, M. 70
Lombardino, L.J. 14
Lubovsky, I. xii
Lunt, I. 6
Luria, A.R. ix, 2

Mahler, M. 143
McCall, S. 44–5, 53
McClenny, C.S. 22, 26
McDevitt, A. 63
Mills, A. 117
Mirenda, P. 119–20, 123

Newman, D. viii, 2
Newson, E. 19
Newson, J. 68

O'Brien 28, 70
Odor, J.P. 145, 151, 157

Painter, C. 60
Pascual-Leone, A. 58
Paulsson, K. 144
Peck, P. 144
Piaget, J. viii, 69–70, 143

RCEVH 44
Ried, B. 15, 17
Rogow, S. 16
Ross, M. 61
Ryan, M. 144

Seligman, M. 67
Shepherd, P.A. 70

Smith, C. 88
Snow, C.E. 14
Snyder–McLean, L.K. 14
Spelke, E. 143
Spencer, S. 61
Stevens, C. xi, xiii
Summers, S. 16–17

Torres, F. 58
Tudge, J.R.H. x, xii

Urwin, C. 16
Uzgiris, I.C. 73

Van Dijk, J. 123
Van Ijzendoorn, M.H. xii
Van der Veer, R. xii
Verburg, G. 144
Verheul, A. 71–2, 83
Vygotsky, L.S. viii–xii, 2, 3, 5, 69

Walker, E.C. 64
Ware, J. 67–8, 71
Watson, M. 145, 151
Watson, J.S. 69
Wenger, E. xii
Wertsch, J.V. 3, 7–8
Whiting, R. 144
Wiesel, T.N. 58
Winterhoff, P.A. xii
Wood, D.J. ix, 8, 41–3, 50–1

Yaroshevsky, M. xiii
Yudovich, F. ix

Subject Index

aims
  educational 4–5, 8, 36, 94, 109
activity design 41–2, 49, 53–5
affordance/afford/affording 7–8, 42, 49
attention
  selective 20, 60, 63
  span 59–60
anticipation 7, 14, 21–2, 32, 38
appropriation viii–ix
assessment
  functional 146–7
  initial 5, 99–100, 133–4
  of communication 6, 17, 88, 132–4
  of developmental level 73
  of likes/dislikes 6, 88, 100–1
  of potential 6, 28, 30–2
  multi-disciplinary 109, 133–4
assimilation viii
auditory scanning 127–8
Augmentative and Alternative Communication (AAC) 116, 118–9, 132–3
awareness 32

braille xi, 44, 58
bubble tube 74, 79–80, 84, 87, 90

cause-and-effect (see also 9, 33, 36, 38, 71, 89, 93–4
  contingency awareness) 97, 120

challenging behaviour 86–8, 90–1, 112–3
child's
  average day/daily routine 6, 133, 136–8
  current abilities 6, 28, 134–5
  potential abilities 6, 28, 135
choice making 4, 7, 10, 34–9, 67, 94, 125–6, 137
collaboration xii, 3, 5
communication
  aids (see also *VOCAs*) 6–7, 10, 29, 116, 119, 128, 139–142, 146
  barriers to 1, 116–9, 136, 142
  effects of technology on xi, xiii
  facilitating viii, 90
  opportunities 20, 138, 141–2, 145–6, 154
  skills 68
  the development of 7, 13–26
    (see also *assessment* of)
concentration 38
concept keyboard 8–9, 41, 44–6, 128
  (see also *touch tablet*)
contingency awareness 69–70 (see also *cause-and-effect*)
contingent teaching 41–3, 48
control (learning to) 1, 7, 9, 33–4, 59–60, 67, 70–2, 92–4, 113, 118, 144
cyclical
  model 4, 10–11

process   132, 135, 146

deafblind (see *multi-sensory impairment*)
defectology   xii–xiii
demand   22, 26
dialogic   ix
digitized sound   41, 43–4

environment
  auditory   57
  distracting   107, 114
  optimal   56, 62
  specific   109
  stimulating   92
  tactile   57
  visual   56–7, 59, 61–2, 92
evaluation (see also *review*)   72, 81, 98, 111, 145, 156–7
expectations   vii, 69, 71, 134
  differences in   135
  low/high   6, 62, 136, 142
  realistic   135

family/families   (see also 71, 80, 82, 133, 136, 138 *parents*)
fibre-optic   74, 84, 87, 90–1, 97
fine motor skills   107–8
finger spelling   xi
functional system   vii, viii, 2–11

generalization   11, 15, 37, 62, 101–3, 106–8, 110
gesture   16, 20–1, 25–6, 29, 36
goal setting   109, 134, 148
grasping   107–8

hand-eye coordination   63
hearing impairment   20, 43, 59–60, 92, 97, 101

improved sensory functioning   57–8, 63
infancy   66–71

intentionality   26, 69, 94, 119
internalization   viii, ix, 3, 7, 53, 69
interpretation   14, 20, 22, 25–7, 28, 69, 81, 85

joint attention   8, 19, 21

language   14, 20, 116–9
latching timer   36, 95
learned helplessness   67, 70, 144
learning difficulty   1, 14, 21, 23, 36, 68, 135, 140 (see also *severe learning difficulties*)
leisure   7, 67, 72, 113
levels of instruction   41–2, 50–2

mediation   vii, ix–xi, xiii, 2, 4, 7, 69–70, 116
messages (design)   8, 10, 122–5, 128, 139, 141
mobility
  augmentative   144–5, 157
  functional   151
Moon   2, 45–54
motivation
  assessment   6, 100, 137
  reduced   67, 70–1, 144
  through choice/control   10, 120, 152
  through joint activities   14, 19
  through sensory experiences   84, 93, 99, 107, 112, 114
  through variety   46
  to explore/learn   56, 144, 146, 153
multi-sensory impairment   xii, 59–60, 92

naming   23, 122–3

parents   17, 68, 73, 80–3, 99, 102, 109, 116, 133, 135–6
pedagogic   vii, viii, xiii
phonics   47, 54
physical disabilities   28–9, 37, 59, 93,

122–3, 127, 135, 138, 143, 148–9
planning 5–8
pleasure 67, 78–9, 93, 100–1, 113
Pragmatics Profile 16–17
Pre-Verbal Communication
  Schedule (PVCS) 15–17
profound and multiple
  disabilities/difficulties (PMLD)
  xii, 66–8, 70–2, 82, 84, 106
programs 36–40
  touchscreen 60, 63–4 (see also
  software)
progression 28–9, 35, 40, 97–8,
  108–10, 140, 151
psychological tool ix–xi

reading 8–9, 41, 45, 52, 54–5
recording 110–11, 148
recording achievement 40
refusal 7, 26
relaxation 8, 71–2, 80, 82, 86–8
request 7, 21, 25, 36, 124, 141
responsiveness 66, 81–2
review, reviewing 10–11, 40, 134–5
rewards 93, 98–9, 107–8, 114
  extrinsic 107
  intrinsic 107
  inventory 100–1
routines 14, 63, 67, 120, 123, 125

scaffolding ix, 8–11, 41–4, 48–9,
  51–5
  physical 51
seating 100, 110, 147, 149
self-stimulation 71, 75–9
semiotic ix–x
sensory
  environment 15, 58, 65
  stimulation 67, 70–1, 100
  stimuli 84
severe learning difficulties 16, 28,
  45, 70, 84, 89, 149 (see also
  learning difficulty)
signing x–xi, 107
Snoezelen 71, 83

social
  development 69
  interaction 66–9, 71–2, 75–8,
    89–90, 121, 143, 154
software 4, 7, 15, 57
  concept keyboard 43–4, 128
  framework 43–4, 64
  single-event 19–22
  sequence 22–5 (see also
    programs)
speech
  and language therapist 20–1,
    24, 36, 99
  digitized 116, 121
  synthesizers 128, 144
  synthetic 57, 59, 116, 121
story 46, 53–5
switch(es) 14, 33–6, 89–90, 95–6,
  104, 112–4, 140–1
switching systems 2, 9, 11, 93–9,
  102–5
symbols ix–x, 29

tactile overlays 41, 44, 46–8, 53–4
taction pads 8, 122–3, 126
talking signifiers 122–3
tape recorder 36, 38, 46, 101, 112,
  120
touchscreen 35, 60
touch tablets (see also 57–9
  concept keyboards)
toys 36, 39, 108
tracking
  tactile tracking 46, 51, 54
transference of learning 52, 58, 62
  (see also *generalization*)

visual
  attention 32, 107–8
  discrimination 64
  impairment 1, 7, 14, 16, 21, 41–
    5, 56–64, 85, 93, 101, 114–9,
    123–9, 135, 146, 148, 155
  skills 62–4, 100, 107
vocalization 20–1, 23, 26, 102,

107, 149
voice output systems/VOCA(s)
116, 119, 122–31 (see also
communication aids)

wheelchair

electric   143–4, 155
powered   143, 151
Smart   143–157

Zone of Proximal Development
(ZPD)   viii–ix, xii, 2–5, 9–11

For Product Safety Concerns and Information please contact our EU
representative GPSR@taylorandfrancis.com
Taylor & Francis Verlag GmbH, Kaufingerstraße 24, 80331 München, Germany

www.ingramcontent.com/pod-product-compliance
Lightning Source LLC
Chambersburg PA
CBHW051745230426
43670CB00012B/2166